Designing US Economic Policy

Also by W. Robert Brazelton

ALTERNATIVE STREAMS IN ECONOMIC ANALYSIS

Designing US Economic Policy

An Analytical Biography of Leon H. Keyserling

W. Robert Brazelton
Professor of Economics
University of Missouri – Kansas City
USA

First published 2001 by
PALGRAVE
Houndmills, Basingstoke, Hampshire RG21 6XS and
175 Fifth Avenue, New York, N. Y. 10010
Companies and representatives throughout the world

PALGRAVE is the new global academic imprint of
St. Martin's Press LLC Scholarly and Reference Division and
Palgrave Publishers Ltd (formerly Macmillan Press Ltd).

ISBN 0–333–77575–9

This book is printed on paper suitable for recycling and made from fully managed and sustained forest sources.

A catalogue record for this book is available from the British Library.

Library of Congress Cataloging-in-Publication Data
Brazelton, W. Robert.
 Designing US economic policy : an analytical biography
 of Leon H. Keyserling / W. Robert Brazelton.
  p. cm.
 Includes bibliographical references and index.
 ISBN 0–333–77575–9
  1. United States—Economic policy—1945–1960.
 2. Keyserling, Leon Hirsch. 3. Economists—United
 States—Biography. I. Title.
 HC106.5 .B713 2000
 338.973'0092—dc21
                                                    00–033328

10 9 8 7 6 5 4 3 2 1
10 09 08 07 06 05 04 03 02 01

Printed and bound in Great Britain by
Antony Rowe Ltd, Chippenham, Wiltshire

Contents

Acknowledgments

The author wishes to thank Dr Benjamin Zobrist, former Director of the Harry S. Truman Library, a Presidential Library, for financial support for the original study of Keyserling and the economic policies of the Truman era. The author also wishes to thank Dennis Bilger and others of the Harry S. Truman Library, Independence, Missouri, USA, for their aid, patience, and cooperation.

Any acknowledgement would be incomplete without a special mention of Dr Willadee Gillan Wehmeyer who worked with me on the original report to the Truman Library on the research project financed by that Library. That project included both an analytical biography of both Leon Hirsch Keyserling and, also, his wife – a respected economist and "feminist" in her own right – Mary Dublin Keyserling entitled: *Leon H. Keyserling and Mary Dublin Keyserling, Growth and Equity: Over Fifty Years of Economic Policy and Analysis, from Truman to Bush*, 1989, Truman Library, Independence, Missouri, USA.

Special thanks go to both Leon Keyserling and Mary Keyserling. Their cooperation was crucial, and the association with them is a bright spot in my memory.

Thanks, also to my typist, Linda Raske; my Doctoral Assistant, Jessie Jo Johnson, whose advice, sincere interest, patience, and pre-editing were crucial. Also, I would be remiss not to mention David Lazarus and the other staff members in Government Documents at the Miller Nichols Library of the University of Missouri–Kansas City for their aid and patience.

Naturally, all errors, oversights, et alius herein are the author's.

Preface

This book is a revision of a previous study, supported by the Harry S. Truman Library, Independence, Missouri, USA, by myself and Willadee Gillan Wehmeyer, a graduate student at the University of Missouri–Kansas City, and now an instructor at Central Nazarene University, Olathe, Kansas.

The Truman Library study involved several interviews, usually of several days in length, with both Leon Hirsch Keyserling and his wife, Mary Dublin Keyserling, in their home in Washington, DC. In the original study, both Chapter I and Chapter II were personal in nature. Chapter I involved the personal recollections of Willadee and myself concerning the Keyserlings. Chapter II involved the Keyserlings' personal stories concerning events, personalities, conversations between personalities, et cetera, that are of great interest to historians and biographers. However, in this book, both chapters have been deleted for a study of the economic events and of economic thought that existed at the time of the Keyserlings' youth; their years of education; and the economic realities of the United States in the pre-World War II and the post-World War II periods. Thus, this specific book is more for economists or economic students and interested lay persons, rather than historians and biographers of the Truman Era. For those who wish to read the original study by Willadee and myself, it is available in Independence, Missouri at the Harry S. Truman Library, Independence, Missouri, USA.

The original copy on deposit at the Truman Presidential Library included both a study of Leon H. Keyserling and Mary Dublin Keyserling by myself and Willadee Wehmeyer. After that study, Dr Wehmeyer completed her Doctoral dissertation on Mary Dublin Keyserling (*Mary Dublin Keyserling: Economist and Social Activist*, University of Missouri–Kansas City, 1994) which expanded upon her contribution to the original work on the Keyserlings. This present work includes only an analysis of Leon Keyserling by myself. The work on Mary Dublin Keyserling will be published separately by Dr Wehmeyer. It is, I believe, an important work in relation to the Roosevelt-Truman eras, and of the women's movement of that and later periods.

W. Robert Brazelton

1
Biographical Background and Analytical Analysis

Leon Hirsch Keyserling was born in Charleston, South Carolina, on January 2, 1908, the son of a prominent Jewish family; and lived his first eight years in St. Helena Island, South Carolina, near Beaufort, South Carolina. His father, William Keyserling, was a prosperous and influential farmer, growing and marketing fruits and vegetables. After Leon Keyserling's graduation from high school in Beaufort in 1924, he went to Columbia University in New York City and became a student of Rexford Guy Tugwell. Later, he received a Law degree from Harvard University before returning to Columbia University to work on his Doctorate in Economics, which he never finished. However, during that time, he was busy helping Rexford Tugwell in his writing; and in doing his own writings. And later, as he often said, he was busy composing and lobbying for legislation concerning the Labor acts, the Housing acts, the Employment act, et alius, which, to him, outweighed a dissertation. Later, he became Vice Chair of the Council of Economic Advisors to the President and succeeded to its Chairmanship after Edwin Nourse's resignation, partly for Nourse's refusal to testify on economic policy matters before Congress – a task Keyserling considered both a necessity and a duty in order to support the President's economic policies before Congress and the Nation.

Keyserling's policies were policies of growth, as will be seen in later chapters. Many economists argue that a growing economy, like a rising tide, raises all ships. Keyserling recognized, however, that some ships would not rise as fast as others or, without aid, may not rise at all. Thus, economic growth was a necessary condition for

1

increasing wealth, but, by itself, was not a sufficient condition. As some sectors of the economy were weaker than others; or, as some groups were weaker than other groups, those groups must be selectively helped by selective policies or selective controls. Thus, anti-recessionary, pro-growth policies should stimulate the overall economy and help lagging sectors as well by selective methods relating to those lagging sectors.

This view of anti-recessionary policy was continued into Keyserling's view of anti-inflationary policy as well. An inflation can be argued to be caused by an excess of demand over supply. This Keyserling translated as a lag in supply in relation to demand. Thus, even though anti-inflationary policy should dampen overall inflationary pressures, it should also stimulate the growth of supply of lagging areas, especially those areas of high priority (for example, housing and the jobs related to housing). Then, even though an anti-inflationary policy may be less lenient than would be an anti-recessionary policy, it must allow for selective sectors to continue to expand via selective controls or interest rates. For example, if housing was in short supply and widgets in excess supply, anti-inflationary policy should restrict the latter, not the former. Also, to Keyserling, the high interest rates caused by anti-inflationary policy were a high cost to the economy and would have to be paid over a long period of time by taxpayers and debtors to bond holders and creditors. Thus, in general, Keyserling believed that interest rates, even in an inflation, should be kept low, and, if increased, only where needed, selectively on a micro level, not a primarily or exclusively macro level.

In light of Keyserling's view of interest rates, Keyserling disapproved of the "Accord" between the Federal Reserve and the United States Treasury in 1951. In the post-World War II, period, the Federal Reserve had "agreed" to purchase Treasury bonds at a set rate of interest. This essentially pegged the interest rate. The interest rate was low and allowed the Treasury to float its bonds without fear of rising interest rates which may be considered as allowing the Treasury to increase debt, which could result in inflation. The reason for this policy was to keep interest rates low; and to belie the fear that the post-World War II years would duplicate the stagnation of the 1930s and the instabilities of the 1920s. However, as expansion – not contraction – was the post-war reality, many believed that such a policy was not needed. Thus, after the Accord of 1951, the Federal Reserve no longer pegged the interest rate which meant that Treasury deficits (bonds) did not have a guaranteed market at a guaranteed interest rate. It also meant that interest rates would likely rise, which Keyserling opposed as an impediment to investment and growth. Thus, to Keyserling, the Accord was an error. To most economists in the 1990s, the Accord was probably seen as a necessity, especially after the large deficits of the 1980s which, without the Accord of 1951, could have been a very inflationary period. Indeed, during the 1980s, both Chairman of the Federal Reserve (Paul Volcker and Alan Greenspan) purposefully allowed interest rates to rise (Brazelton, 1993; Cebala and Koch, 1989; Neikirk, 1987) to limit economic growth and to cause the recession of 1990–91 (Hall, 1993) in order to prevent inflation. It should be pointed out that Keyserling, in the period 1946 to 1953, was reacting to that particular period of time in US economic history and would have never dreamed of such large fiscal deficits as in the 1980s.

To a modern economist, the concept of the Federal Reserve pegging the interest rate low to provide cheap funds for the Federal deposits may be difficult to understand. However, one must remember that economists in the post-World War II period were still being influenced by the Great Depression of the 1930s; and many economists feared the return of that depression after the end of World War II. Thus, they wished for a stimulative policy after 1946. After a mild inflation in 1949 and the Korean War, the fear of a return to depression had become minimized and the Accord was the result. In the following chapter, we will analyze some major economic analyses of the Depression years; the years in which the Keyserlings were being educated and the world they saw around them with its economic stagnation, high unemployment, homelessness, and social strife. This was to influence both Keyserlings and it was to forge their views concerning both economic and social policy – economic growth for economic welfare for all.

Thus, the questions to be analyzed in this specific work relate to the theoretical background of Leon H. Keyserling himself: the major aspects of his economic analysis; the major policy goals derived therefrom; and his importance in relation to the "liberal" agenda of the time, of which he was a major player.

Keyserling believed that the major work of John Maynard Keynes (later Lord Keynes) – *The General Theory of Employment, Interest and*

Money (1936) – was an important work in the development of relevant economic analysis, especially after the advent of the "Great Depression" of the 1930s. However, Keynes' stress in *The General Theory* was upon an economy at less than full employment. Keyserling's stress was upon economic policies that would get the economy to full employment, and would then allow the economy to grow at a full employment rate of growth via economic policies and incentives (micro and macro) – both demand-side and supply-side policies. These policies would be in terms of an adequate money supply; low interest rates; tax policies; investment policies; and selected incentive policies towards selected, crucial, lagging sectors of the economy as needed. In relation to the latter, Keyserling was of the firm belief that economic growth must be balanced. That is, on the macro-level, if demand is growing, so must supply. If supply is growing, so must demand. On the micro-level, if the demand for steel is growing, its supply must be growing as well as the products and processes that supply the steel industry. This is a problem of eliminating or preventing bottlenecks to full employment and its long-term continuation. These problems will be discussed in greater detail in the chapters that follow.

Keyserling began his significant influence upon economic policy as early as the first administration of President Franklin Delano Roosevelt (1933–45). It continued into the following administration of President Harry S. Truman (1945–53), especially in relation to the Council of Economic Advisors (CEA) to the President, of which Keyserling was the first Vice-Chair and the second Chair. Afterwards, Keyserling remained a critic of the economic policies of subsequent presidents via his numerous testimonies before the Joint Economic Committee Hearings of Congress (HJEC); speeches; the production of "Conference on Economic Progress" (CEP) pamphlets; and other writings to be analyzed in the chapters that follow.

Thus, the following chapters will discuss and analyze the life's work of a remarkable man – Leon Hirsch Keyserling (1908–87). However, in terms of an analysis of his life's work, we will end this chapter with a brief review of his more major contributions, via the Memorial Service in his honor on September 10, 1987, which shows the respect in which he was held by friends and colleagues.

After Leon H. Keyserling's death on August 9, 1987, I had the honor of an invitation to his Memorial Service on September 10,

1987, at the Cosmos Club in Washington, DC. Those who spoke in honor of Leon H. Keyserling helped to sum up the accomplishments of his life; and to put his life into historical perspective. I would like to close this brief chapter on Keyserling's work and the economic and political history that he represents by quoting remarks from selected mourners at the Memorial Service who, as I did, knew, worked with, and respected this man of action, brilliance, and dedication.

After recounting the accomplishments and virtues of Keyserling, several of the speakers spoke of his belief in the ability of the economy to give a good life to us all; and in the ability of the social system to achieve more equity and well-being – in part, through continued economic growth shared by everyone.

One of the first to speak was Congressman Augustus Freeman Hawkins of California (a joint author of the 1978 Humphrey-Hawkins Act) who indicated that Keyserling, at discussions with colleagues, would stress the historical record before reaching the crux of his argument, at which time his colleagues knew that he must be right about the economy and its needs (Keyserling, Mary Dublin, 1987, p. 10, Memorial Service).

Congressman Claude Pepper of Florida stressed Keyserling's nobility, compassion, intellect and concern for all Americans; and his desire for a better America shared by all Americans (Memorial Service, p. 21).

On the academic side, Michael Harrington, Professor of Political Science, Queens College, stressed that Keyserling always remained optimistic and confident about America and its future potential. To Harrington, Keyserling was part of the essence of the New Deal/Fair Deal. To Harrington, the death of men like Keyserling points out the lack of such men of courage to oppose the "politics of reaction" [my words] and the intellect to develop new ideas for that opposition (Memorial Service, p. 19). That such courage was lacking in 1987 was obvious to most of those present at the Memorial Service and, to this author, remains lacking in the present era, 1999 to 2001.

More specifically, on the political side, Senator Paul S. Sarbanes stated:

> Leon himself was a person of steady vision and extraordinary vigor. His commitment to the strengthening of the economy in order to build a better society never wavered for one minute over

the course of eight decades of his extraordinary life ... Leon was a
thinker, a doer, a fighter for what he believed to be right, an
American with a profound faith in the American people and in
the nation's future. Above all, he was a deeply moral man.
(Memorial Service, pp. 16, 18)

More specifically, on the academic side, John Kenneth Galbraith of
Harvard University stated:

We remember at this meeting this afternoon one of the truly
committed and effective leaders in modern economic policy and
beyond ... on all compassionate economic action and reform. I
decline to believe that men like Leon Keyserling are of the past. I
believe or assuredly hope that they are also of the future.
(Memorial Service, p. 16)

To that, I can only say: "Amen."

2
Influences of the Times:
The 1930s

The post-World War II period from 1919 to 1930 is sometimes referred to as the "Roaring Twenties": which gives the impression of prosperity. However, it was only roaring for some. There was a difference between the affluent characters of *The Great Gatsby* and the poor in *The Grapes of Wrath*. The 1920s saw fluctuations in economic activity; and the 1930s saw the Great Depression upon which conservatives looked with fear and the Marxians with hope. To demonstrate the socio-economic and political influences on the era of the 1930s (the time when the Keyserlings were becoming active in political circles), I will choose two economists to set the stage. The first is Alvin Harvey Hansen (1887–1975) who influenced many economists such as Paul Samuelson (Nobel Prize in Economics, 1970); David McCord Wright; James Duesenberry; and John Kenneth Galbraith. Hansen, after he became a Keynesian, set the tone of economics and of economic policy until the early 1960s from his position at Harvard University (Brazelton, 1993). Thus, Hansen will be used to set the general tone of the times. The second, Rexford Guy Tugwell (1891–1979), was an important influence upon Leon Keyserling himself, as the study at the Truman Library (Brazelton and Wehmeyer, 1989) indicates in greater detail than is necessary here.

Hansen began his academic career as a Classical economist. As a Classicalist, he had a strong belief in laissez-faire, if the latter was not disturbed by the presence of monopoly or monopsony, or other market imperfections (Brazelton, 1993). After his academic move to

Harvard and after his Presidential Address to the American Economic Association on the economic effects of declining population growth (Hansen, 1939), Hansen became a Keynesian (Brazelton, 1993). Hansen may, however, be said to have been more pessimistic than Keynes and stressed fiscal policy over monetary policy more than Keynes might have, but, nevertheless, Hansen was the leading advocate and interpreter of Keynes in the United States along with some others such as Abba Lerner.

Hansen developed what has been called by some the "Keynes-Hansen Stagnation Thesis," although Hansen and Keynes had no correspondence concerning it; thus, it is, in reality, a stagnation thesis developed by Hansen based partly upon Hansen's analysis of US History and, partly upon Hansen's interpretation of Keynes.

To Hansen, the American economy had in the nineteenth century developed significantly in economic terms because of three underlying growth factors: the rapid growth of population; the opening up and development of the Western frontier; and the adoption of new technology.

The rapid rise in population growth in the nineteenth century was a result of both domestic births and immigration. The growing population kept the labor supply young and, as a result, net consumers; and it kept labor-wage pressures low.[1] It also enabled the filling up of the Western frontier with new farmers, new miners, new railroad workers, new western urban dwellers, et cetera. Indeed, even after the end of the "geographic frontier" in 1889–90, the eastern capital from such financial centers as Boston, New York, Philadelphia and Baltimore could be invested in the process of Western urbanization that lasted into the 1920s. Then, too, the new technology from the days of Samuel Slater, to Eli Whitney, to Henry Ford, and many others kept US markets competitive and US output varied for internal consumption and production and for external demand (exports) (Brazelton, 1961, 1993, 1994). In Hansen's view, these growth factors all began to decline after World War I.

To Hansen, the rate of population growth (Hansen, 1939); the Western frontier and its urbanization; and the rate of technological innovation (as separate from invention) declined, all simultaneously. The result was the Great Depression of the 1930s. The policy implications were the development of theories of monetary policy and fiscal policy by such economists as Alvin Hansen, Alba Lerner, and others. Finally, in 1946, this resulted in the Employment Act, which established (1) the federal government's obligation to maintain high employment; and (2) set up the Council of Economic Advisors to the President of which Keyserling was the second Chair. Thus, Hansen influenced the economic analysis and the monetary–fiscal policy implications of that era, as well – an influence that is still operative today.[2]

Rexford Guy Tugwell was a more direct and personal influence upon Keyserling. Tugwell was one of Keyserling's first professors at Columbia University in New York; a mentor to Keyserling during his graduate economic studies (after Keyserling's law degree from Harvard). Tugwell was instrumental in taking Keyserling to Washington after the election of Franklin Delano Roosevelt in 1932. Tugwell was to stay in Washington as Assistant Secretary of Agriculture. Later, after 1937, he was appointed Governor of Puerto Rico and Tugwell was, according to John Kenneth Galbraith, an early supporter of the first elected Governor of Puerto Rico, Munoz Marin, who, as Governor, was one of the initiators of "Operation Bootstrap" which made Puerto Rico the most advanced economy in the Caribbean (Galbraith, 1981, pp. 176–7).

Tugwell and Hansen did differ in areas of social and economic policy. Whereas Hansen believed economic stagnation occurs in capitalist economies, he also believed that stagnation and/or business cycles could be offset by countercyclical monetary–fiscal policy, especially fiscal policy. Hansen thought that monetary policy was less viable, especially in a depression, because of a misinterpretation of Keynes by many American Keynesians concerning the possible flatness of the money (liquidity preference) demand schedule in a depression (Brazelton, 1961, 1993). Tugwell, on the other hand, would go further than Hansen. Tugwell believed, as would Hansen, that the newly emerging structure of the socio-economic system of capitalism precluded both old theories, (such as the laissez-faire of Say's Law) of capitalist economic analysis, and old economic policies. Tugwell further believed, however, that a form of central economic planning was essential to the survival of the type of capitalism that had evolved from the eighteenth century to the twentieth century. As a new system had evolved, the concept of instrumentalism (as espoused by John Dewey) demanded new economic policies as well. Thus, Tugwell would go beyond Hansen's adherence to countercyclical economic policy and also espouse economic planning.

To Tugwell, an economist should ask not only what the trend in economics is, but also what it should be; and what the individual economist can do concerning what should be (Tugwell, 1935, p. vii), using both deductive and inductive reasoning (ibid, p. x). Tugwell also believed there had been in the past – the Greek period (500 to 300 BC) and the Medieval period – what he referred to as "golden ages" where something like an approach to socio-economic equilibrium had occurred, but these had occurred before the development of the modern, industrial city and of industrialism itself (ibid, pp. 372–3). Thus, to Tugwell, a modern economic "equilibrium" must consider complex, cultural, historical and industrial forces, which are complexly and delicately interrelated (ibid, p. 373). Furthermore, and very optimistically for the future of man, until the Industrial Revolution (1750) and the economic abundance it brought, Tugwell reminds us of the historical fact that in the past, mankind was at the disposal of nature and its changes. However, to Tugwell, after the industrial revolution, nature had become the servant of mankind, not the master. This fact was a significant difference between the past and the present–future (ibid, p.374). Thus, the machine and nature can be exploited, not man himself as man had been in previous history. Now, the "Smiths, and Browns and Joneses, common folk" could share in the economic surplus that was no longer enough for just the few. Thus, the "common folk" now have a desire, a stake, and an obligation to control the forces that shape their lives. However, Tugwell believed (as did Keynes) that superstition and rationalizations had become both prevalent and dangerous in that they prevent the correct policies from being understood and initiated. Thus, education has become more important due to the complexity of the socio-economic system; the evolving nature of the system; and the increasing difficulty of carving out a living on the homestead (family farm) than ever before (ibid, pp. 378–9). This meant, on the national economic level, that economists must change as well.

If Classical theory is to be refuted and left in the past, what type of economics, to Tugwell, should replace it? The answer is "experimental economics" free from the "inertia of traditionalism." The goal of economics must not be micro self-interest and profit, but social welfare as defined by Jeremy Bentham (ibid, p. 395). Also, there must be a realization that there are no certainties and absolutes. As the socio-economic system evolves, the illusion of certainties and natural laws must give way to the real world of uncertainties and expectations.

For example, Tugwell believed, as did his pupil Keyserling, that economics had inherited a bad reputation and odor from its past analytical history that only a complete revision of economics could solve. The economics generally taught in classrooms was, to Tugwell, largely non-relevant to the real world. What was necessary was for economists to undertake experiments (not abstract general-izations) to solve the problems of society and its parts (ibid, p. 384). Furthermore, American economists, to Tugwell, have an obligation to inform the public as to what the American economic system (or any economic system) both could do and should do; and to point the economy towards the goals to be achieved (ibid, p. 384). This point was not lost on Keyserling.

Tugwell had more negative criticisms of the economic profession of his day; and there is a strong probability that he would similarly criticize the economic profession of today. He asserted, for example, that economic theories are theories reflecting a pre-industrial age, not an industrial age – diminishing returns, iron law of wages, value theory; and a false belief in an analogy between natural law and socio-economic laws. Economic laws were not, to Tugwell, "natural laws" as they had become under Classical economic analysis where such laws had become ends, not processes to find socio-economic policies for a better world for all. The "natural laws" had become a means to justify the state of affairs that existed, not what could be accomplished. To him, truth would be useful, but Classicalism was not truth! (ibid, p. 393).

To Tugwell, the fact that man is merely an economic animal (as in Classical economics) interested only in pecuniary gain, is socio-logical nonsense. Tugwell points out that throughout human his-tory, such concepts as altruism, tribalism, patriotism, family values, race, sex have at times overwhelmed purely economic motives of profit and individual gain; or existed simultaneously alongside such pecuniary self-interest as discussed by Adam Smith in the latter's analysis of "the butcher, the brewer, or the baker" (ibid, p. 408). To Tugwell, man is more than an economic agent; man is a social agent as well.

So far, in our discussion of Tugwell, we can see his desire to over-throw the constraints of "natural law" and Classical economics built upon it; to replace the economic view of man as an economic maximizer (*homo economicus*); and to develop an economic analysis and policy that allowed for experimentation (experimental economics) based upon research and upon man's rational use of that research. Economists must use quantitative tools, actual socio-economic measurements, unless they wish to continue "blindly" as before (ibid, p. 415).[3] To Tugwell, industry in the age of surplus for (in Tugwell's analogy) the Smiths, Browns, and Joneses and the common folk holds great promise for the future of mankind. However, if economics is to make mankind truly free to achieve economic good, economic science must take into consideration the realities of the industrial age and its production enhancing benefits; and economics cannot be merely a summation of theoretical concepts. It must instead, be "experimental economics" (ibid, p. 422).

But what is industry now? And what is a rational economic policy to be in light of what industry now is? Tugwell explored these questions as well. In beginning to answer those questions, Tugwell starts by analyzing war. He points out that wars between industries and firms (which have many of the attributes of nations) and wars between nations are both deleterious. But as long as firms, business, industry, or nations are organized as they are, wars between them will be inevitable (Tugwell, 1932, p. 75). Thus, the business–goverment concept of laissez-faire is obsolete as industrial wars must be prevented if economic science is to continue to increase the welfare of the whole – the Joneses as well as the Vanderbilts.

Also, to Tugwell, the Classicalist concepts of self-interest, competition, and laissez-faire are counterproductive to profit, despite the Classicalists rationalization to the contrary. Competition, laissez-faire, self-interest can be ruinous to profits, as the Great Depression of the 1930s proved to Tugwell. Instead of the competition of the Classicalist variety, Tugwell substituted the concept of national planning. Planning, to him, can minimize "risk," minimize "weeds" in the economic system, and maximize "successes" when the framework of a national plan whose aims are known; whose benefits and beneficiaries are known; and where risk and uncertainty are no longer – as under laissez-faire – the potential destroyers of profits, companies, and economies. Planning substitutes industry as a "game" for industry as a "rational product" of and for the society as a whole, not merely for the individual gains of the industrialist (ibid, p. 76). Notice that both the role of business and the role of government has changed. Business no longer is competitive and self-interested as in the Classicalist tradition; but is cooperative. Government is no longer reactive or laissez-faire, but proactive in terms of planning for the good of all the society. The role of profits is also changed; no longer are profits an accidental furnisher of funds (gains) or destroyer of funds (losses) via individualist decisions based upon inadequate information. Profits become part of the plan, not an accidental consequence of the uncertain and unpredictable market. Speculation for profits (which can destroy profits when the decisions of individuals are in error) is substituted for the plan of which profits are a part. However, to Tugwell, as later to growth theorists such as Evsey Domar and Sir Roy Harrod, production increases necessitate consumption increases. Thus, to Tugwell, planning involves more safety for all. Planning involves safety for the producer and is, thus, generally supported by producers. However, once it is realized that planning for production also involves planning for consumption, planning becomes less supported. Planning for production does not consider prices so that producers may limit production to give a satisfactory price to them and to profits. But planning for consumption involves fair profits and wages for consumers to consume – production is for the purpose of consumption. When it is realized by businesses that planning involves production, and, also, consumption and prices, as well, they become less favorable to planning (ibid, p. 83). However, a macro-economic crisis or micro-economic losses of a firm may be caused by production–supply exceeding consumption–demand. Thus, both must be considered, as Keyserling was to later emphasize. Thus, to Tugwell, planning is the opposite of conflict (ibid, 1932, p. 89); and involves a downgrading of merely pecuniary business gains for a "civil service loyalty and fervor" (ibid, p. 90).

So, for Tugwell, laissez-faire must be abandoned and a planned industrial society must be established. To the possibility that such might threaten profits and, thus, business, Tugwell argues that such would help to guarantee profits; and that many industries distribute their profits to agencies that had done little to earn them, so that profits were not as clear a causation as the Classicalists and their assumptions of self-interest and revenue maximization had assumed.

Two questions now emerge. What does this mean to Tugwell? And what influence did it have upon Keyserling? The first question is more difficult to answer than the second. Tugwell has, I believe, an unrealistically optimistic view of the benefits of planning; and the social manipulatability of mankind. The recent collapse of the Soviet Union and of "Stalinist Centrist" planning are indications of this fact. However, that is criticizing Tugwell in the 1990s concerning what he wrote in the 1930s when the US economy was in a depression and the Soviet economy seemed to have promise in increasing output, growth, and in changing human, social behavior. However, in Tugwell's favor, it can also be said correctly, I believe (perhaps emphatically) that the Soviet experiment with central planning went too far and/or was perverted by the Communist leaders themselves or Communist ideology itself from being a long-term success. Indeed, it seems that Tugwell would have never gone as far as did the planners of "Stalinist Centrism." He did criticize planning on merely a "predictive level" as useless for business persons who would have no reason to follow or believe the predictions of the planners; and he did mention Gosplan (ibid, p. 83), but it is unclear as to whether or not he would have copied Gosplan. There are, after all, many levels of planning between the extremes of laissez-faire and Gosplan.

Keyserling was influenced by Tugwell. This came out in Keyserling's backing of the Employment Act of 1946; his acceptance of monetary–fiscal policy; his backing of the Humphrey-Hawkins Act of 1978 (which postulated for the United States a type of planning similar to French "indicative planning" but which has not been implemented to any significant extent by the Reagan–Bush administrations (1980–92), nor by the Clinton administration (1993–2001); and his view that full employment assumed an increase in production and an increase in consumption, and, thus, also, a rational increase in wages and employment to help tie together production increases and consumption increases so as to maintain the long-term growth of the macro-economy. However, whatever Keyserling took from Tugwell, Keyserling also kept his own pragmatism. Thus, however far Tugwell may have wished to go, Keyserling would be pragmatic in terms of analysis and policy. This pragmatism is a key to Keyserling's views of the world. As Alonzo Hamby (1973, p. 301) says of Keyserling:

> Economic policy should concentrate less on prices as such and more on the relationship between wages, prices, and profits; it should work for the optimum balance between consumer

purchasing power and corporate income in order to maintain full employment and expansion. The New Dealers, he believed, had turned too frequently towards controls to fight inflation. Selective controls might be necessary at times, but the way to deal with inflation was to enlarge productive capacity to meet demand.

The above quote emphasizes Keyserling's stress on economic growth of national income to enrich all, rather than the redistribution of income between classes. This tenet became central to his credo as a liberal. Indeed, Alonzo Hamby summarizes both Keyserling's criticisms of the New Deal of the Roosevelt era as compared to the Fair Deal of the Truman era. To Keyserling, according to Hamby, the New Deal had underestimated the economic task of ending the Depression of the 1930s and, thus, never did enough fiscal–monetary stimulus (until, of course, World War II with its large increases in military expenditures). Also, the New Dealers had become too adamant concerning anti-trust policy and the return to competition. They did not recognize, in Keyserling's opinion, that bigness in some industries was necessary; was more cost efficient in some industries; and that the complete competitive markets' structure of Classical economic theory (even if such "competitive" market structures may have never existed in fact) could not be completely restored even if such a restoration were desirable. Third, to Keyserling, Keynesian economics was more fitted *politically* [my emphasis] to anti-recessionary policies than to the less popular tools of anti-inflationary policy (lower expenditures and/or higher taxes). Lastly, New Dealers had lost their confidence in capitalism itself, which Keyserling and his interpretation of the Fair Deal never did. In relation to the latter, Hamby states:

As Keyserling envisioned it, American capitalism had virtually unlimited opportunities for growth; an ever-expanding economy could produce undreamed-of abundance and material gain for all classes. The liberals should concentrate *not* [my emphasis] on reslicing the economic pie but *rather* [my emphasis] on enlarging it. Business could expect higher profits, labor better wages, farmers larger incomes, and, above all, those at the bottom of the economic scale could experience a truly decent life (ibid, 1973, p. 300; see also, pp. 297–303; 172; 332–3; 415–18; 447–8; 453–4 for Keyserling's policies and his interpretation or the liberal credo based upon economic growth, not redistribution). (Note, also, that the above, in terms of sales and profits of business, higher incomes of workers through higher wages are interrelated on the macro-economic level.)

Note, in the above, that Keyserling recognized the role of profits; but also, the relation between profits, wages and between the private and the public sectors. These relationships and their maintenance and changes over time, were essential to obtain and maintain long-term economic growth. Also, to Keyserling, inflation (price increases) was less of a problem than depression and unemployment and with an appropriate balance between prices, wages, profits, et cetera, inflation could be minimized (ibid, p. 301). Indeed, to Keyserling, as we will analyze later, inflation was more of a problem of inadequate supply rather than excess demand, a belief that was central to Keyserling's policy prescriptions up to and including the Korean War (ibid, pp. 447–8; 453–4).

Based upon the above analysis, it is now time to turn from the influences upon Keyserling and his times to a consideration of the analysis and policies of Keyserling himself. The following chapters will do this in terms of economic analysis; economic policy, and his economic testimonies before Congress that will cover most of five decades.

3
Leon H. Keyserling and the Council of Economic Advisers

1946 – Edwin Nourse, Chairman; Leon Keyserling, Vice-Chairman; John D. Clark

1949 – Leon Keyserling, Acting Chairman; John D. Clark

1950 – (midyear) Leon Keyserling, Chairman; John D. Clark; Roy Blough

Introduction

As World War II reached its closing months, many economists began to worry about the economic future of the United States. The war years from 1939 to 1945 had seen American prosperity grow as US factories produced the military goods to defeat the German and Japanese forces. However, prior to the war the world economy had suffered from a decade of depression in the 1930s following the stock market crash in 1929 and the banking crisis in 1933. These events followed the economic problems of the 1920s. Many economists believed that the post-World War II era would witness a return to depression. Their belief was based upon the fact that the period preceding the war had been a time of depression and that post-war periods usually saw recessions as military expenditures declined. They felt that what was true of previous post-war periods would be true of this one. However, these economists overlooked two factors. One was that the domestic war prosperity had built up consumer savings which were awaiting the purchase consumer goods after wartime rationing and after wartime production controls were lifted. The second factor was that post-war economic policy was going to direct the economy in such a way that the free market system would not return to the Depression of the 1930s. Much of this latter effort was due to Leon Keyserling and the Council of Economic Advisers to the President (CEA).

As the war years came to a close, the Pabst Brewers developed the idea of an essay contest relating to post-war economic policy. One of the winners of that contest was Leon Keyserling with an essay entitled "The American Economic Goal: A Practical Start Toward Postwar Full Employment." The essay began by stating:

> This war has awakened Americans to the promise of America. We are now producing goods at a rate more than 50 percent higher than during the best years before the war and when peace comes, we shall have millions of our finest manpower, drawn from men and women in our armed forces, to add to our production forces – if we have the brains to make room for them. We shall have a chance to abolish poverty, to reach higher standards of living than ever before. We can set the example to the world, by solving economic problems underlying so many wars (Keyserling, 1944, p. II).

The essay called for the establishment of a Congressional Committee whose chairperson would be appointed by the President. The tasks of the Committee would be four-fold. First, it should recommend an "American Economic Goal." Second, it should advertise this goal. Third, it should outline the task of achieving the goal by both the public and private sector. Lastly, the tools of wartime economic control should be "retained, altered or abandoned to help achieve the American economic goal in accord with the greater freedom and flexibility of the American Economic Policy." (ibid, p. 12). It was Keyserling's firm belief that correct post-war economic policy would prevent the recessions that had followed most wars in the past. The prevention of such a recession would allow the servicemen to come home to employment, prosperity and security rather than unemployment, poverty and an insecure future of wasted lives and human resources (ibid). To Keyserling, such a plan would not only maintain prosperity, it would also be a bulwark in defense of liberty, free enterprise, and democracy against the totalitarian forces that bred upon unemployment, wasted lives, unused resources, and human poverty.

Thus, Keyserling became an early proponent for what was to become the Employment Act of 1946 that set up the Federal responsibility for maintaining high employment and economic stability and established the Council of Economic Advisers to the President, a council that Keyserling would serve on from 1946 to 1953.

The Employment Act

The Employment Act of 1946 did not spring solely out of the immediate post-war period. It had its roots in the period following the economic calamities of the 1929 to 1933 period which had brought Roosevelt to power and such persons as Keyserling to Washington after the election of 1932. As Robert J. Gates (1968) pointed out in a thesis entitled *The Role of the First Council of Economic Advisers*, the early theoretical analysis to back the Employment Act came from such persons as John Maynard Keynes and Alvin H. Hansen in the 1930s (Gates, 1968, p. 10). By 1940, the National Planning Association had been formed "by a few reformist intellectuals, but it also gained active participation and interest from a handful of business representatives, by labor organizations, and by national agricultural associations" (ibid, p. 11). As the end of World War II drew near, the Senate Postwar Planning and Economic Committee, the National Housing Agency, the Department of Agriculture, the Department of Commerce, the Department of Labor, the Office of War Mobilization and Reconversion, and the Bureau of the Budget became interested in the goals of post-war full employment (ibid, p. 13); so did such prominent individuals as Budget Director Harold Smith; Chairman of the Federal Reserve Harold Eccles; Secretary of Agriculture and later Vice-President Henry Wallace; and such legislators as Congressman Wright Patman (D, Texas); Senator James Murray (D, Montana); Senator Joe M. Kilgore (D, Texas); Senator Robert Wagner (D, New York); Senator Elmer D. Thomas (D, Utah); Senator Joseph O'Mahoney (D, Wyoming); Senator Wayne Morse (D, Oregon); and others (ibid, p. 215). The bill, first referred to as the Murray Bill, was originally under the jurisdiction of the Banking and Currency Committee of the Senate. The Murray Bill was considered to be giving too much power to the executive branch, not adequately defining full employment, and being the first step towards economic regulation of the nation (Ibid, p. 24). The result was a compromise. As such, the Employment Act of 1946 passed the

House on February 6, 1946, the Senate on February 8, 1946, and was signed by President Truman on February 20, 1946 (ibid, p. 27). The objectives of the Act were to promote "(1) employment opportunities for those able, willing, and seeking work; (2) promotion of maximum employment, production and purchasing power; (3) deference to other needs and obligations and other considerations of national policy ..." (ibid, p. 28). There were, however, some limitations to the Act. The Act maintained a commitment to the free enterprise system; it provided for technical assistance in determining price and employment policies; and it maintained the right of the President and Congress to make policy decisions (ibid, p. 29). Lastly, of course, the Act created the Council of Economic Advisers, a council upon which Keyserling was to serve as both the first vice chairman, and, later, as the second chairman until the end of the Truman Presidency in 1953.

As the Employment Act stipulated, there were three members of the Council of Economic Advisers: Edwin Nourse, Leon Keyserling, and John D. Clark. Nourse had been associated with the Brookings Institute, the American Farm Economic Association, and the American Economic Association. Clark had been a lawyer for the Midwest Refining Company and vice-President of Standard Oil of Indiana and, later, was to be Dean of Business at the University of Nebraska. Keyserling had graduated from Columbia University and later Harvard Law School. He had taught at Columbia University as a doctoral student. After the election of 1932, he had served in the Agricultural Adjustment Administration, the United States Housing Authority and the National Housing Agency. Earlier he had been a legislative assistant to Senator Robert Wagner of New York (ibid, pp. 38f). Keyserling's economic, legal, and political background set him in good stead to help solve some of the earlier problems of the Council of Economic Advisers.

There were some problems both before and after the passage of the Employment Act. The first was the term "full employment" itself. The second was the availability of the President to the Council; and third was the role of the members of the Council in the formulation of policy and testifying in front of Congress.

The first problem was over the term, "full employment". What did such a term mean? How could *full* employment (of everyone?) be achieved? *Could* such a goal be achieved? Was it desirable to achieve such a goal even if such a goal were possible? Would the achievement of such a goal be inflationary? Due to the questions and due to conservative opposition, the term "full employment" was substituted for the phrase "conditions under which there will be afforded useful and remunerative employment opportunities, including self-employment, for all Americans who are willing to work and are seeking work" (ibid, p. 35). Thus. the legislation that passed Congress in 1946 was a statement that stressed free enterprise, but that maintained that the Federal government had some responsibility in maintaining "maximum employment, output, and purchasing power." It was, indeed, a victory for the so-called liberals. As Alonzo Hamby points out, there were two primary schools of thought concerning the management of American economic policy after World War II. One school believed in "an engineer-managed economy run for production rather than profit," whereas the "liberals," fearing facism and bureaucratic control instead:

> advanced a much smaller, though highly significant, role for government – the manipulation of tax policy and the use of government spending to raise puchasing power and supplement private investment until the economy reached full employment. Its goal was a competitive capitalism freed from both excessive government control and the ravages of the business cycle ... (Hamby, 1973, p. 9).

The liberal view was the Employment Act of 1946, the view of Keyserling. Once again, this goal of Keyserling's is summed up in the prize-winning Pabst essay:

> The American Economic Committee should define an American Economic Goal, reflecting America's optimum productive capacity, national income and employment, and correlating these with an optimum standard of living within the reach of American families. The Goal would be a continuing inventory of our needs and resources – with subgoals reflecting major categories.
>
> This Goal would involve neither regimentation nor compulsion. Democratically conceived by a representative committee, it would express America's voluntary sense of its power and promise. We would not proceed towards it under the forced draft of war "quotas." We would move at whatever pace the people approve.

To achieve this Goal, American enterprise and government, whose tools have proved superb in producing for war, would function in peacetime under greater freedom and flexibility, but equally clear purpose and determination, of an American Economic Policy.

The Committee would present the Goal to the public, in a brief, popular report, signed by Committee members and approved by the President. Thus, the driving force toward the Goal, focusing continually upon the performance of both enterprise and Government, would be that prime weapon of democracy, the watchful eye of an informed people. (Keyserling, 1944, pp. 14f)

There are several points that the Keyserling essay demonstrates. First, the commitment to the primary role of the private sector in income, output, and production. Second, the commitment of the Government via its policy goals toward maintaining the economy at a high level of economic activity, but without regimentation and with an informed public. Third, the controls of the World War II war-time economy would be dropped for the more subtle controls of monetary and fiscal tools within the framework of free enterprise, the American Economic Goal, full employment, but without regimentation. Fourth, implicit in the Keyserling Pabst essay and implicit in the early Reports of the Council of Economic Advisers, was the concept of the Full Employment Budget which was later popularized by Walter Heller under the presidency of John F. Kennedy (Brazelton, 1978). Fifth, there is the possibility that Keyserling would have gone one step further, with the adaptation of "indicative planning" as utilized by post-war France. This supposition is supported by his contacts with French planners; his later writings; and his support of the Humphrey-Hawkins Act in 1978 which put into law the possibilities of indicative planning, an act which was, to Keyserling, largely ignored by the Council of Economic Advisers under subsequent Presidents and Congresses.

The second problem confronting the Council of Economic Advisers was the problem of contact with the President. Edwin Nourse, the first Chairman of the Council of Economic Advisers, desired an office in the West Wing of the White House but was given an office in the Executive Office Building – near, but not in the White House (Gates, 1968, p. 41). Nourse had wanted White

House offices in order to have close contact with the President. Nourse was disappointed with his contacts with the President on economic matters. For example, in a letter quoted by Corinne Silverman, Nourse stated that his interview with President Truman only lasted 30 minutes, which suggested to Nourse that the President was uninterested and that the Council would have no significant influence on the development and adoption of the President's economic program (Silverman, 1959, p. 5).

Keyserling, however, as pointed out by Silverman and Gates, refutes Nourse's contention. Keyserling argued that the allegation of Nourse that President Truman had not been considerate to him (Nourse) was extremely unfair in that Nourse could see the President at any time; and that Nourse did not realize the actual nature of the Presidency – a very busy office with many national and international problems. Thus, the President, as Keyserling pointed out, did not have time to engage in a lengthy "bull session" on economics such as those at the Brookings Institute where Nourse had previously been an Associate (ibid). The President wanted facts and policies, not lengthy, theoretical discourse.

The problem of whether or not the President was accessible to the Council chairman introduces a third problem – the problem of the role of the Council. Nourse believed that the Council should be advisory to the President. However, to Nourse, the Council members, including the chairman, should not be required to testify before the Congress, including the Joint Economic Committee. Nourse believed that testifying before the Congress would introduce the Council of Economic Advisers into the "political arena." Also, Nourse believed that it would be embarrassing if he had to support a Presidential decision with which he did not agree or which he had recommended against (Gates, 1968, p. 48). The other members of the Council differed with Nourse. Keyserling, for example, always believed that he should advise the President, but that he should support the Presidential decision before Congress or anywhere else. He should argue his disagreement to the President but not in public. The President was, to Keyserling, the President. If one strongly disagreed with the policies accepted by the President, he should resign first, and then, publicly criticize. Nourse wanted to avoid the issue by not testifying. President Truman temporarily solved the problem by instructing Nourse to allow the other two members of the Council – Leon Keyserling, the vice chairman, and John D. Clark –

to testify. In the future, both Clark and Keyserling testified, but Nourse did not. After the election of 1948, Nourse resigned from the chairmanship. In the first draft of his letter of resignation to the President (a draft which was revised and did not include the following), Nourse wrote that if the Economic Council was to be assigned a political role; to stray into political activities; or to be subject to political influences, he (Nourse) would not serve as the Chair and would want to be relieved of these responsibilities at once (Silverman, 1959, p. 8). The President obliged.

In a way, to Keyserling, Nourse was trying to be in two worlds simultaneously. Keyserling and Clark both felt that they were the President's economic ambassadors to Congress. Keyserling felt that Nourse was contradicting himself when he refused to testify before Congress, but then openly criticized the President in public. Nourse argued that before a Congressional Committee, he could not choose his subject matter, but in public he could (Gates, 1968, p. 52). The infighting was not unnoticed by the Congress. The Congress reduced the Council's budget in two successive years. Many Congressional leaders shared the view that the chairman of the Council of Economic Advisers was duty-bound to testify on economic matters and on economic policies of the Administration before the appropriate Congressional committees. The Council of Economic Advisers, like it or not, was part of the political arena. Keyserling recognized this. Nourse did not. The question is succinctly stated by Robert Gates:

> This controversy was basically – should the Council act as an economic supreme court dispensing pure economic science or should the Council participate freely in the political process? Should the members testify before Congressional Committees? Should they seek support of the President's economic programs or make public speeches in support of the President's program, et cetera? Dr. Nourse's position was, briefly, that of the "ivory tower" attitude which stressed the anonymity of Council members as personal and professional advisers to the President. Mr. Keyserling's position, however, was a much broader interpretation of the Act. He felt that the Council should be involved in the political process (ibid, p. 61).

After the resignation of Edwin Nourse in 1948, Leon Keyserling was appointed as Acting Chairman of the Council of Economic Advisers

and, finally, as Chairman of the Council. The position of chairmanship for Keyserling was a controversial decision. Although Keyserling had studied economics at Columbia University (including all
doctoral graduate economics courses except his dissertation) and
had been associated at Columbia closely with Rexford Tugwell, he
did not have a doctorate in economics. He had helped in the
writing of some of Tugwell's works; had been an attorney in the
Agricultural Adjustment Administration; a general counsel and,
later, Acting Administrator of the United States Housing Authority;
and legislative assistant for Senator Wagner (D, New York), a powerful Senator and close ally of Franklin Roosevelt. Nevertheless, some
felt that he should have a doctorate in economics (a point later
brought up, somewhat inaccurately, by President Reagan in relation
to John Maynard Keynes). Keyserling, who continued to criticize
academic economists because of their "ivory tower" attitudes and
their later fascination with mathematics (instead of economics)
believed that his work in the political and economic area of the
Roosevelt Administration was far more important than a doctoral
dissertation on some obscure subject. Indeed, I personally have
heard major professors say to their students, in essence, to finish
their dissertations and then, to forget them. A dissertation is a
research tool, not a career. Others agreed with Keyserling and supported his selection as the replacement to Edwin Nourse as chairman of the Council. Indeed, as Gates indicates, Edward Flash points
out the absurdity of this objection to Keyserling's appointment.

Flash contended that there was no basis for an objection to
Keyserling as chair of the Council. Simply stated, Keyserling's
16 years of government service had prevented Keyserling from following the traditional academic pathways while he was involved
with actual problems of economic policy, socio-economic legislation, economic stabilization and growth, full employment, et
cetera. To Flash, there were few American economists with that
much time and expertise devoted to public policy, including a
working knowledge of the responsibilities of the Council of
Economic advisors and the Employment Act – an Act which
Keyserling had proposed; helped to author; and lobbied Congress to
pass. That Act had, furthermore, established the Council upon
which Keyserling had served as its first Vice Chair. In other words,
what else was logically and reasonably needed (Flash, 1965, p. 27) to
make Keyserling a prime candidate for the position?

Keyserling was, of course, confirmed by the Senate and served the Truman Administration until the inauguration of Dwight Eisenhower in January, 1953. Keyserling had sharp differences with the former chairman, Edwin Nourse, over the role of the Council of Economic Advisers. As Robert Gates points out, "the conservatives viewed the Act with emphasis on the free enterprise system, while the liberals saw the broader aspects of the Act – particularly in terms of expansionary policies" and economic growth (Gates, 1968, p. 56). As we shall see later, this resulted in a sharp contrast between the Economic Reports to the President under the chairmanship of Edwin Nourse (1946–49) and those under Leon Keyserling (1950–53), and later those done for Dwight D. Eisenhower.

The real crux of the matter was not, of course, free enterprise versus a planned economy. The conservatives and the liberals were both interested in the preservation of free enterprise, especially in light of the bureaucratic controls of the recently defeated fascist Germany and the controls of "Stalinist Centrism" in the Soviet Union. The conservatives, however, thought mainly in terms of counteracting swings in the business cycle as such swings occurred. The liberals, such as Keyserling, certainly stressed counteracting the short-term business cycle, but they also concentrated on the long-term growth of the economy. This involved the overall planning of Federal taxes and expenditures over time, but did not involve the planning of individual, private sectors of the economy. Low interest rates in the housing industry would, for example, stimulate construction of new homes by the private sector without the interference of the public sector in the construction of middle-class housing. Such a policy has made the United States perhaps the best housed middle-class in the world. We have not, as Keyserling pointed out, done as much for the lower classes. That point we will return to later. In a letter to President Truman, Dr Nourse summarized these philosophical positions concerning the role of the Council of Economic Advisers:

On the one side are those who still look to the Employment Act, even in the form in which it was finally accepted, to launch the Federal Government on a comprehensive and continuous program for engineering optimum performance by the whole economy and who expected the Council of Economic Advisers and the Joint Economic Committee to draw blueprints for that program and keep them continuously revised. On the other side are those who understood the Act as merely stating a broad objective or ideal towards which effort should be directed and as introducing additions to our executive and legislative institution which would aid the economy – both in private and public sectors – in moving more competently toward that goal. (Colm, 1956, p. 62)

Nourse believed in the latter view. Keyserling leaned toward the former view, but the terms of "engineering" and "blue prints" probably go beyond Keyserling's policy thinking, partly because he believed that economic matters were not that precise. Nourse tended to believe in hard money and was generally against the Fair Deal. Nourse was for tighter Federal Reserve control, whereas Clark was not. Keyserling was for the Fair Deal and felt that wage–price guidelines were at times necessary.

Indeed, as Flash pointed out (Flash, 1965, p. 23) and as this author can ascertain, it was said of Keyserling that he was a person of ability, dedication, ambition; and a prodigious worker; and one who could be both cooperative and irritating – sometimes simultaneously! However, he was also said to have a missionarial heart, a political ego, and a strong desire and ability to lead the fight for the right and for justice for all (ibid, p. 23). This was, of course, evident in his economic policies aimed at the concept of economic growth for the benefit of all Americans.

My own feelings concerning the personality and dedication of Keyserling are similar. However, I found him to be a person with an immense sense of humor – sarcastic and pointed at times, but never malicious. One of his quips was often worth much more than a hundred pages of written history or analytical economics. He could get quickly to the heart of the matter and preferred it that way. Alvin Hansen pointed out that Lord Keynes was, in private, a similar type of man (Brazelton, 1987). These men, and women, tend to get things done. Indeed, when Keyserling became Chairman of the Council, economic growth became the major emphasis of the Council. This can be seen from the historical record below.

The historical record of the Council, 1946–53

1946 – Edwin Nourse, Chairman; Leon Keyserling, vice-chairman; John D. Clark

1949 – Leon Keyserling, Acting Chairman; John D. Clark
1950 – Leon Keyserling, Chairman; John D. Clark; Roy Blough

The first report of the Council of Economic Advisors (CEA) was submitted to the President on January 8, 1947. It was an optimistic document pointing out that 1946 had achieved the high employment level of 58 million jobs, 10 million more than in 1940 and higher than the wartime peak (CEA, 1947a, p. 1). Unlike the predictions of many economists, a post-war recession had not occurred (ibid, p. 2). There were two million unemployed but production was 50 percent above 1939, although this was 15 percent below the wartime peak (ibid, p. 1). The policy was to maintain maximum purchasing power. In this report, one can see an early Keyserling influence. To Keyserling, the economy was to have maximum purchasing power, as he believed total output was related to consumption, GNP = f(C). Keyserling would point out that without consumption, investment would not be forthcoming. The purpose of production, to economists and producers, was consumption and profits came from consumption. Also, the report pointed out that a key to the future was the relation of wages, prices, and profits. Since the end of World War II (V-J day), prices had risen by 3 percent by mid-1946 (ibid, p. 2). However, by the end of 1947, the consumer price index had risen by 15 percent – food, textiles, housing, construction – and wages had risen 10 percent (CEA, 1948b, p. 4). Thus, if there were a problem, it would be inflation, not recession. However, the Council's anti-inflationary policy was not to restrict demand, but to increase output. In fact, this is a key to Keyserling's economics – growth and expansion. The key to solving inflation is not high interest rates, but more investment to increase output. High interest rates impede investment. The Federal Reserve should put a primary emphasis upon monetary aggregates, not interest rates. Of course, discretionary changes in the growth of the money supply eventually affect interest rates, but more slowly, and, thus, with less anti-investment effects. Another key is here, too, as Keyserling was pro-housing, he would also be pro-low interest rates which encourages housing starts since interest is a major cost to the builder and, especially, the buyer. Also, to Keyserling, housing could be used as a policy tool – increased housing starts in a recession would not only house people but it would also employ workers in housing and related industries.

In the long term, then, the goals for 1947 were to increase production by decreasing bottlenecks caused by shortages in some sectors of the economy. However, even if bottlenecks were eliminated, there still would be the problem of labor and management disputes over wages and other labor-management problems. In 1946–7, as now, the price–wage labor problem remained, as Paul Samuelson (Samuelson, 1951, pp. 412–19) indicated, a most significant unsolved problem of capitalism (and if the Polish economy and the Chinese economy are included as of 1989, of socialism, too) (Brazelton, 1977). However, the 1947 *Report* indicated that since the Federal government would have a budget surplus and business was saving for investment, the consumer would have to take up the resultant slack in aggregate demand by borrowing or using past savings (CEA, 1947a, p. 10). This was likely to happen as the pent-up consumer demands festered from World War II and the preceding recession, especially in such areas as consumer durables. Indeed, the 1947 *Report* felt that the price of consumer durables would rise until an increase in their supply drove prices down again (Brazelton, 1977, pp. 10f). As 1946 consumer disposable income was $1,026.00 per capita, significantly above the 1935–9 high of $497.00 and prices were 39 percent above the 1935–9 average, disposable income had risen faster than prices. This was favorable for consumption (ibid, p. 12). Savings also had declined (1944 = 28 percent of disposable income; 1946 = 9.5 percent of disposable income) (ibid, p. 13) to increase consumer demand – a favorable prospect. However, if the price rises of 1946 continued into 1947, inflation could result. Thus, the *Report* warned:

But undue extension of deficit financing on the part of millions of American families can gravely hurt our business system and lead in the end to deficit financing by the Government. In the long run, consumers must rely on current incomes for purchasing power (CEA, 1947a, p. 13).

The 1947 *Report* then listed some policy objectives for the future. First, remove wage–price controls left over from World War II with the promise that business would reduce prices where possible. Second, raise the minimum wage. Third, increase the use of antitrust legislation to prevent pricing abuses. Fourth, increase social security benefits to support purchasing power of consumers. As there were one million new housing units needed in 1947, increase housing by 6 billion dollars in 1947. In good times, budget revenues should exceed expenditures. In bad times, revenues should not exceed expenditures (the concept of the cyclically balanced budget). Lastly, reduce taxes *equitably* to maintain purchasing power. The *Report's* emphasis upon purchasing power, a minimum wage, price reductions, deficit financing in a recession, and lower taxes to maintain purchasing power were most likely due to Keyserling's influence. To Keyserling, the secret of maintaining GNP was high consumption, where, to him, GNP = f(C). A more succinct analysis of the economic theory of Keyserling can be seen in Chapter 7.

The 1947 *Report* (CEA, 1947a) also indicated other long-term goals. The first was the retraining of the labor force. Next was to maintain family farms and to keep farm incomes equitable to those of the rest of the economy. However, agricultural price supports should not be too high so as to perpetuate maladjustments. Also, as there was a connection between labor productivity and labor health, there must be health care available to all. There must also be a backlog (shelf) of public works ready to be started if national income should decrease.

The *Midyear Report* of 1947 (CEA, 1947b) picked up on the decline in inflation. Prices had leveled off during early 1947 except in the coal industry where wages were increasing more rapidly than productivity (ibid, p. 2). Thus, coal prices were still rising which meant an increase in steel prices (ibid, p. 3). So the coal-steel sector was still inflationary, but the rest of the economy (especially textile, leather, and electrical appliances) was beginning to decline even though purchasing power still remained high (ibid, pp. 3, 11f). The *Report* (CEA, 1947a) emphasized the need for price reductions to stimulate demand instead of wage increases (ibid, p. 20). The Council pointed out that price reductions benefited all consumers, whereas wage increases benefited only those powerful enough to get them. If the more-powerful received wage increases and the less-powerful did not, this was an inequitable redistribution of income determined by market power, not economic efficiency (ibid, pp. 20f).

The 1948 *Report* indicated the continuance of prosperity. Consumption was still up and the economy was maintaining the record level of' 60 million jobs. Production was 7 percent above that of 1946 and 76 percent above the average, 1935–9 (CEA, 1948a, pp. 1–2). Purchasing power had begun to decline, but disposable income in 1947 was $1,264.00 compared to $1,074.00 (adjusted) in 1946 (ibid, p. 2). A decrease in savings had helped to bolster consumption. However, price increases had hurt the low income groups. The budget was in surplus (5.6 billion) and housing starts were double those of 1946. Total investment was also above 1946 (ibid, p. 3). Times were good. The economy was still strong. The policy recommendations reflected these facts.

The policies suggested were: continue present taxes; reduce the federal debt with the current surplus; continue rent controls and housing starts; increase the minimum wage and social security benefits to strengthen consumption; restrain credit creation; allocate scarce resources to needed sectors; consume and develop natural resources and expand the productivity of human capital (ibid, pp. 5–7) and restore the Federal Reserve's right to regulate credit (ibid, p. 48). However, in relation to the Federal Reserve, the *Report* indicated that if there were shortages in the economy or even inflation, rationing would be better than price increases (ibid, pp. 48–51). Rationing, the argument went, did not disemploy people, higher prices caused by shortages and inflation do. This point, of course, goes back to Keyserling's belief in growth, not restrictions, to maintain the economy and to avoid inflation. It would be better to ration in case of shortages in certain sectors of the economy (and then expand that sector) rather than stop the growth of the entire economy through fiscal or monetary policies. As the *Report* stated, "our whole history shows that unless we go forward, we shall slip backward, our economy should be stable, but nonetheless it must continue to grow" (ibid, p. 53).

The *Midyear Economic Report* of 1948 (CEA, 1948b) was less optimistic. Inflation had not moderated, but increased. The *Midyear Report* suggested an excess profits tax to restrain inflation and for a treasury surplus. It suggested a greater reliance on consumer credit controls and bank credit controls. It did recognize that the credit–inflation problem was not unidirectional. The increase in the supply of credit could stimulate inflationary pressures, but, also, the inflation increased the demand for credit. However, the inflation could not continue as, eventually, inflation limits expansion through higher costs and uncertainties. Thus, a policy of government control was considered necessary as voluntary controls do not work unless everyone assumes that everyone else will act reasonably. When recent history indicates that groups have been acting unreasonably, it is not rational to believe that they will suddenly begin to act reasonably. What has occurred in the recent past biases one's perception of the future (ibid, pp. 45–9).

Inflation continued to be a problem analyzed by the 1949 *Midyear Economic Report*, but the possibility of a recession – the first post-war recession – was also discussed. It was pointed out that employment and production had remained high in 1948. On the plus side, price increases had decreased and food prices had fallen. On the minus side, some wages had risen faster than others and the coal and shipping strikes had been disruptive. Profits were up, which was good for business, but the question of other reinvestment was raised in terms of maintaining aggregate demand. Still, both consumption and investment were increasing. Housing starts were still increasing, but at a decreasing rate. Part of the decline in housing was due to price increases in housing (CEA, 1949a, pp. 4–6). The export surplus was declining and the budget surplus was still acting as an anti-inflationary control. The expansion of bank credit had been slowed by both voluntary restraints and by restrictive policies (ibid, p. 5).

The goals for 1949 were simple. Prosperity was to be continued and inflation was to be prevented – another hint that the Council was aware of the inflationary possibility. There were to be programs for housing, health, education, but not at an inflationary pace. There was to be a better balance between investment, consumption, wages and profits on the belief that economic stability and equity are compatible – a point often stressed by Keyserling (ibid, p. 9). Also, the nation should continue its defense systems and continue its program of domestic development and welfare plus international development. There was a dual stress on both security and freedom (ibid, p. 9).

The policy recommendations included a fiscal surplus and stability on the government bond market to maintain public confidence. At this time, the Federal Reserve was maintaining a bond rate of 2 1/2 percent. In relation to the recommendation that the Federal Reserve maintain this rate, there was also the recommendation that the Federal Reserve be allowed to maintain its power to change reserve ratios and installment credit, an authority which was due to expire on June 30, 1949 (ibid, Introduction, p. 11). Also, if shortages were to develop to cause bottlenecks, selective controls in terms of prices and allocations were to be utilized. Once again, the Council felt that selective controls to prevent bottlenecks was a superior policy to higher interest rates which would recess the entire economy. If the problem were micro (particular parts of the economy), the solution need not be macro (the entire economy). One of the shortages suggested was in the area of electric power. Also, it was suggested to develop the St Lawrence Seaway Project to cheapen transportation rates to the Midwest and the Great Lakes states (ibid, p. 15). Housing was still in too short a supply so the recommendation was made to maintain rent controls until the shortage was over (ibid, p. 13), but not forever.

Inflation was still a problem even if the Council had mentioned the possibility of a recession. Nevertheless, in terms of the inflation, the Council desired to protect those whose incomes had lagged behind the increases in living costs. To this end, the Council recommended: an increase in Old Age and Survivors Insurance; the extension of the Fair Labor Standards Act and an increase in the minimum wage from 40 cents an hour to 75 cents an hour; public assistance to the less fortunate; farm supports, but one that allowed farmers to shift from one product to another, the concept of resource mobility; slum clearance; education and national health insurance; and, internationally, an International Wheat Agreement, European Recovery, and reciprocal trade agreements, all to increase US exports and, thus, US employment (ibid, pp. 14–18).

The 1949 *Report* indicated some theoretical analysis. The concept of balanced growth appeared. Also, there was a another germ of what was later to become the so-called "Full Employment Budget" of Walter Heller under President Kennedy and the later Humphrey-Hawkins act of 1978.

In terms of balanced growth, the Council report indicated that defining objectives is not the same as establishing blueprints for a regulated economy. Defining objectives was, instead, merely establishing benchmarks for policy needs and for business needs (ibid, p. 50).

The Council report of 1949 also stressed consumption once again. Consumers, according to the Council, should consume 75 percent (at that time, consumers consumed 70 percent) of the GNP in order for prosperity to continue and to absorb private savings and federal surpluses. To Keyserling, as indicated before, the distribution of income was an important problem, not only to equity, but also to stability. One way of maintaining high purchasing power for maintaining prosperity was via housing and its influence on the purchase of consumer durables. One reason for the emphasis upon increased consumption was the Council's prediction that as post war-time shortages disappeared, investment would decline from 15 percent to 11 to 12 percent so as to balance new production with ongoing consumption (ibid, p. 61). The Council's essential question concerning anti-inflationary policy in view of the possibility of a recession can be assessed from the following quotation:

> Our analysis shows that over the ensuing years consumer income and expenditures should be increased both absolutely and relatively. The fundamental issue is: will the increase result automatically through the interplay of prices and costs on the market place? Or will a depression appear when the gap between potential output and effective demand of consumers and business becomes unmanageable as has happened in the past? Or can affirmative policies, as envisioned in the Employment Act, close or bridge the gap before it becomes a chasm? (ibid, p. 74)

The above question points out both the use of the full employment budget (gap between potential output and effective demand) by the Council, and their assessment if the dangers of a recession should occur. To the Council, a deep recession in the 1940s would be less dangerous than one in the 1920s. The reasons are several: better policy information; social security; farm programs, and other "built-in stabilizers" that will help to minimize the economic shocks and to lessen the destruction of liquid assets. However, the Council pointed out that if prices become sticky or if they decline, business may become pessimistic. Price and wage adjustments are necessary and wages must move to sustain consumption and the output of investment. But two questions arise. First, when do price decreases make businessmen pessimists about the future? Second, when do wage increases become deflationary by adding too much to costs? There needs to be a balance between consumption, prices, costs, and production (ibid, p. 75). Thus:

> The important organized groups within the economy, such as business, labor, and agriculture, need both the economic analysis and the practical machinery which will enable them better to harmonize their separate interests with the common good and to compose even if not completely agree upon these matters which

from a narrower perspective might seem irreconcilable. (ibid, p. 75)

Minimum wages adjusted to prices will help in that compromise between labor and business, as will social security, and housing programs. Indeed, to Keyserling, housing could be utilized in recessionary times as part of a shelf of public works. Overall, the 1949 *Report* indicated that "The upward adjustment of consumer incomes relatively to prices will be essential in the future to establish sustainable patterns of balanced economic growth" (ibid, p. 76). As prices increased, wage earners needed to be able to afford to buy or else recession would occur.

The *Economic Report* of January, 1949, was mainly aimed at inflation, but hinted at a possible recession. The *Midyear Report* of 1949 indicated the reality of that recessionary fear in what was described as "A moderate downward trend ..." (CEA, 1949b, p. 3). There was a decrease in employment from 61.3 million in 1948 to 59.6 million in 1949 with a 1949 unemployment level of 3.2 million, or 6 percent as compared to 3.4 percent. Wholesale prices had declined 9 percent compared to a 3 percent decline in consumer prices; but profits had declined by over 13 percent below the first half of 1946. Wages had continued to increase, but this had been offset by less overtime and a shorter work week. Real earnings, thus, were about the same. Farm incomes declined by 8 percent (ibid, p. 3). However, counteracting those negative trends, the cash payments of the Federal government rose 20 percent; state and local expenditures were up 13 percent; and federal receipts were down 10 percent, but state and local receipts were up 5 percent. In all, the combined effect of state, local, and Federal budget was a cash deficit. The Federal deficit was about 1 billion dollars as compared to a surplus of 12.1 billion dollars in 1948, both measured for the first half of the year. Thus, governments *en toto* were engaged in anti-recessionary economic policies (ibid, p. 4). However, the Council had some more specific policies to aid in the anti-recessionary efforts.

The specific policies were several: a repeal of the transportation tax; liberalize the tax carry-over for losses; raise estate and gift taxes; lengthen the loan maturities of the Reconstruction Finance Corporation, increase farm supports; increase the amount and duration of unemployment compensation; raise the minimum wage to 75 cents an hour; extend readjustment allowances to World War II veterans; increase old-age and survivors insurance; help states locate sites for useful projects; and restore the Reciprocal Trade Agreement Act (ibid, p. 13); and concentrate on areas of serious unemployment (ibid, p. 12).

The economic decline of 1949 was not projected to be a serious long-term problem. Investment was down, but much of the decline in investment was due to surplus goods. The question became: After the market absorbed these gluts, would investment increase once again? To the Council, the answer to that question depended upon profits. The Council Report suggested that if firms tried to maintain per unit profits and, thus, avoid price decreases, the recession could worsen. To the Council, lower short-run profits or even losses were better in terms of long-run adjustment policy and, thus, in terms of long-term business and employment economic health. This was, of course, a "Neo-classical" form of economic analysis, not the "liberal" political tradition. However, it points out a problem in economic analysis. Neo-classical economic analysis assumes the complete flexibility of prices, wages, profits, interest rates, et cetera. In a recession, prices were to fall to stimulate aggregate demand. If prices did not fall. consumers could not buy more. Thus, the recession was worsened, or lengthened. If a firm tried, then, to maintain its current per unit of profits, it would try not to reduce prices, but this would prolong the recession (ibid, p. 9). So short-term per unit losses brought about by lower prices might increase aggregate consumer demand quicker and. thus, end the recession quicker. The sooner the recession ended, the sooner profits and expansion could be continued. If the economy were controlled by groups which limited price flexibility, the economy would not automatically adjust. This was, of course, a key to Lord Keynes' reasoning behind the causes of the Depression in the 1930s and the failure of "Neo-classical" economics to explain that crisis. To Keynes, the system had lost its automatic adjustment mechanisms regardless of how well they had or had not worked in the past. The *Midyear Report*, 1949, put it quite succinctly:

> What price adjustments will prove feasible and helpful must be considered in close connection with wage and other income adjustments. Price reductions add to real income only if consumers' money incomes are not correspondingly reduced. This leads to special concern for protecting those major sources of

income upon which demand so largely rests. The attempt to secure lower prices through wage cutting would clearly be damaging at a time like the present when consumption demand is proving inadequate and business slack is developing. A sound first rule to apply now is that the general level of wage rates should at least be maintained. (ibid, pp. 7f)

The recession did end. Part of this was due to the active policy called for in the Employment Act. Part of it was due to the size of the Federal government in the 1940s and, thus, its influence on the overall economy as compared to the 1920s and the 1930s. The government sector was crucial to the overall economic growth and stability of the economic system.

The 1950 Presidential Message and Economic Report to Congress pointed out the end of the 1949 recession and the contributions of both the public and the private sectors in doing so.

This effective teamwork between free enterprise and government confounded the enemies of freedom who waited eagerly, during 1949, for the collapse of the American economy. Our economy continues strong. We are able to continue and advance the domestic and international programs which are the hope of free peoples throughout the world. (CEA, 1950a. p. 1)

But maximum employment and maximum production are meaningless terms unless they are turned into policies that mean more jobs and more business opportunities in each succeeding year (ibid, p. 2). They are also not static, one time goals, but dynamic goals in a growing economy over time.

The above quote indicates three important things. First, that cooperation between the private and the public sectors had reversed the recessionary tendencies. Second, economic policy must be adjusted yearly because: (1) economic conditions change from year to year; (2) as the labor force grows from year to year, so must employment opportunities grow from year to year; and (3) as output grows from year to year, so must aggregate demand, private and public, to consume that increased output. But if output is growing and if demand must grow to consume that output, a third problem arises – the problem of economic balance. That problem, the Council also attacked in its *Report to the President*. To the Council:

> achieving a sustainable balance among the various sectors of our economy ... requires that production and incomes shall not develop in a manner resulting in the periodic downturns we have witnessed in the past. (ibid, p. 2)

Thus, it does make a difference what wages, prices, and profits are doing in the economy as a whole. If prices were not flexible downward, increased purchasing power must come from wage increases out of productivity increases. However, all wages should not move simultaneously. The movement of wages must depend upon productivity trends. If wages rise slower than productivity rises, profits will increase but, eventually, consumption will fall to recess the economy. If wages rise faster than productivity, profits will fall so as to eventually decrease investment. Both profits and consumption are necessary in continuing economic growth and economic health. The balance between profits–wages and investment–consumption respectively is not unimportant (ibid, p. 100). High consumption is the key to continued economic health – a concept constantly stressed by Keyserling. In relation to this belief, the Council, via the Presidential Address, had several legislative proposals. To the Council, the correct policies would be to stimulate business and to increase consumption through a reduction in tax inequities; increase housing for the middle income groups; increase the maturity length for Reconstruction Finance Corporation loans; keep farm incomes up and provide for shifts in farm production via payments to farmers; liberalize social security; increase grants in aid to States; extend rent controls for one year (it was recognized that an increase in rents could decrease consumption in the long run, but a long-term rent control could prevent housing construction starts); begin the Columbia River Valley Authority and the St Lawrence Seaway; approve the International Trade Organization; maintain import–export bank guarantees; and increase Federal Reserve power over bank reserves. All of these programs would help the consumer to consume goods for long-term economic growth and add to the ability of the public sector to influence that growth via positive economic action toward maintaining profits and consumption (ibid, p. 16).

The period from 1946 to mid-1950 were times of peace. However, on June 25, 1950, President Truman sent the Air Force and the Navy to Korea in response to the North Korean invasion of South Korea. On June 30, the President authorized the use of ground and air attacks against North Korea. The Korean War (June 1950 to July 1953) had begun. Economic policy was forced to change. In his economic address to Congress, the President indicated that military funds and output must increase, especially the correct forms of output. The general policy stress was to be an increasing output to fight the Korean conflict. However, the Council did make some specific recommendations which were also announced by President Truman so as to maintain the economy, but to prevent excess profits from decreasing overall economic growth and economic equity. The policy suggestions were to eliminate the reduction in the excess profits tax and to increase corporate taxes from 20 percent to 25 percent. Taking into account the 20 percent surtax, this would increase corporate taxes to 45 percent for profits over $45,000. Also suggested was to increase individual tax rates from 15 percent to 18 percent. They were also to restrict credit to prevent an increase in the demand for and prices of scarce materials, especially materials needed for the war effort as well as to give loans and other incentives to increase the production of military goods. These policies showed a realization of the need to increase output, especially of military goods. The policies also indicated that tax revenues were needed to pay for these military goods and to avoid the inflation that night be caused by fighting the war by means of low taxes and high deficit spending (CEA, 1950b, p. 14). In the *Midyear Report*, even if full mobilization is necessary, "price, wage, manpower controls should be avoidable" (bid, p. 41). The reason stated was that "there is some margin of unused capacity in most industries, even apart from the use of double shifts and overtime work, and there is still a substantial reserve in the labor force" (bid).

The Korean War ended the discussion concerning the preceding recession. Employment rose. In 1950, Gross National Product rose by over 5.6 percent of what it was in 1949. Industrial production in 1950 rose to 18 percent more than June, 1949. In terms of index figures, given an index of 1935–1939 = 100, the index of production rose to 199 which was 2 percent greater than the 1948 postwar peak of 195 (ibid, p. 53). It seemed that the level of military production could rise without cutting back on domestic production.

By mid-1950, the Korean War had not yet influenced prices significantly. However, food prices had risen as had tin, lead, textile and chemical prices. Also, there were wage pressures, especially in construction (ibid, pp. 61–3). However, due to the five year wage contracts in the coal industry and the Chrysler Corporation, work stoppages and wage pressures would diminish in those areas of production (ibid, pp. 57–62). Disposable income rose by 5.5 percent and consumption rose by 2.0 percent. The difference was absorbed in consumer debt repayments, liquid asset accumulation, and payments on new homes (ibid, pp. 98–9). However, while optimistic, the report also began to look again at the inflationary threats by stating:

> expansion of the last six months has rested not only upon the shift from inventory liquidation to accumulation, and upon the payment of the extraordinary veterans' dividend, but also upon factors of more lasting duration. Prior to the Korean development, it was to be expected that the economy, during the rest of the year, would continue to move towards maximum employment and production in a steady manner. Since then, the request for additional military appropriations, and greatly accelerated consumer and business buying, have resulted in an increasing threat of shortages, price increases, and other inflationary developments. (ibid, p. 99)

The January 1951 report stressed the need to increase production of military arms for the US and its allies plus an increase in domestic output. Military budgets were close to 20 billion dollars and projected to reach up to 55 billion dollars which also meant that an additional 8 percent of the labor force would be under arms or in munitions (CEA, 1951a, p. 2), as the war threatened to increase its demands upon total national output from 7 percent to 18 percent (as compared to a high of 45 percent in World War II, but, nevertheless, a current drain on the use of domestic resources). The need for steel was increasing from 103 million ingots to 120 million. Steel capacity was seen to be too small and was projected to grow by up to 30 percent over its pre-war levels (ibid, p. 4). Employment was 8 million over the peak year of World War II; output per man hour was up 10 percent, and capacity was growing (ibid, pp. 3–4). However, there was some inflation. As the war had started when the economy was closer to full employment than in 1940, capacity pressures began sooner and, thus, inflation. By late 1950, wholesale prices were up 15.5 percent, and in textiles by 24 percent (ibid, p. 6). It was seen as necessary to balance supply and demand and to set supply priorities for the war effort. All must sacrifice. Consumers would have to postpone consumption. Taxes would have to be equitable. Workers must work at necessary tasks, not necessarily the most enjoyable tasks. Thus, there were several priorities. The Defense Production Act of 1950 set these priorities: a priority for defense; an attempt to distribute non-defense goods equitably; provide needed resources; conserve such resources as aluminum, cobalt, cadmium, copper, nickel, rubber, tin, and zinc; accelerated amortization and direct loan requests to needed areas; set aside agricultural allotments and put price supports at 90 percent; the training and recruitment of unmarried women for the labor force; longer labor shifts; a health emphasis for workers and soldiers to increase productivity; a drive for more doctors; an attempt to balance the budget with increased wartime taxes; and, via the Federal Reserve Regulation W and X, higher down payments and shorter repayment periods on consumer installment loans; price ceilings on autos, steel, copper, lead, zinc via negotiations with business and labor interests. Wages were seen as the heart of family income, but they need not be controlled if prices were. A Wage Consultation Board was to consult with all interested groups (ibid, pp. 13–21).

The Council report indicated the consumer hoarding of rubber and sugar based upon the memories of rationing during World War II. The Federal Reserve raised the rediscount rate and bought government securities to stabilize the interest rate on government securities. There was a modest budget surplus in 1950, but prices were rising and, thus, increased taxes and controls were seen as necessary. In November 1950, the Chinese intervention in the Korean Conflict meant that peace was a long way off and that military expenditures and military conscription must rise – a 100 percent increase in the draft was foreseen (CEA, 1951a, p. 34). Consumers were bidding up prices. The Federal Budget was close to balance, but bank credit had increased (ibid, p. 40). If the economy went into greater inflation, the Economic Stabilization Commission would have to go into wage–price controls (ibid). The policies were aimed at manpower, the industrial base, and maintaining services to consumers and producers (ibid, p. 63). When 600,000 to 700,000 persons reach working age, an increase in labor force would increase output (ibid,

p. 64). The increase in the labor force was seen as necessary as longer hours alone would probably decrease productivity (ibid, pp. 70–2). There was the hope that wartime expenditures plus needed consumer expenditures could both be obtained through economic growth – a key to Keyserling – but if the war increased into total war, many materials, including steel, would have to be reserved for military uses only. As steel was already in short supply, an increase in its capacity was called for, plus an increase in the ore carrying capacity on the Great lakes or an increase in iron ore imports from Labrador and Venezuela (ibid, p. 75), putting a new emphasis upon the St Lawrence Seaway project.

Despite the Korean War and its utilization of resources that otherwise would have gone into domestic production for domestic consumption, Keyserling, now as chairman of the Council, still stressed growth, rather than domestic retrenchment, to provide the goods for the military and for the domestic economy. The report in several places indicated this emphasis on growth.

> The expansion of our national output, with selective emphasis upon vital lines of production, will help to ease the immediate burden of our enlarged defense objectives. In the longer run, production, and more production, is the most fundamental economic remedy. (ibid, p. 77)

> The main reason for the seriousness of the inflationary problem, however, is not that we are now weaker but rather that we are now stronger than we were then. Being more prosperous now, we have less room to undertake new burdens without generating inflationary pressures. If we are unwilling to convert the strength underlying this greater prosperity to meet the new challenge now confronting us, that strength would become a liability rather than an asset. But if we are willing to channel that strength – of tools and manpower and skills – we shall find ourselves now better able than ever before, and far more able than in 1940, to measure up to the responsibilities imposed upon us by world events. (ibid p. 79).

Later, after discussing such matters as a balanced economy, plus needed priorities and anti-inflationary efforts and the need for equity, the report went on to say that:

The early experience during World War II afforded eloquent proof that the greatest obstacle to overall efficiency was the slowness in developing a useful and comprehensive programming operation, and locating it ultimately at one point of authority. (ibid p. 85)

and further,

There will be no problem in inducing the expansion of purchasing power, but instead one of restraining the growth and the use of purchasing power. Maximum production will be even more vital than in peacetime. But the major problem here will not be to devise national economic policies to furnish incentives, markets or capital to private enterprise, in general, but instead to channel our limited resources of manpower and of materials into lines of production which are most essential. (ibid, p. 86)

There were several specific policies suggested by the wartime Council (ibid, pp. 87f). These were for the expansion of selected industries; the expansion, training and health of the labor force; housing, agriculture; atomic energy; and to pay for the war by taxes, not deficits, to decrease inflationary pressures. The Council report stressed the need for tax equity, but recognized that the lower and middle classes would pay most of the taxes due to their numbers – for example, in 1951, it was estimated by the Council that 86 percent of tax revenues came from those with less than $10,000 in annual income (Ibid, p. 104). However, estate and gift taxes on the wealthier might make the burden more equitable, plus an excess profits tax. The credit markets must also provide needed funds to maintain investment and liquidity, but credit policy needed to restrict funds to more vital needs to prevent inflation through such means as the Federal Reserve controls such as X, W regulations (ibid, p. 109). A wage policy must also be devised to hold costs down; to restrain purchasing power in some sectors; to attempt some approach to equity; and to provide for consultation between the interested parties. What Keyserling always seemed to have had in mind was some mixture of the Swedish wage–productivity policy and French indicative planning with an emphasis on growth. Growth was the key to both economic prosperity and political stability.

The July *Midyear Report* of 1951 continued the growth-orientated view of the Council's January report. In the Presidential Address, there was the mention of expansion and stabilization and that whereas second quarter 1950 output had been 300 billion dollars, the second quarter of 1951 was 330 billion dollars in real terms (CEA,1951b, p. 11). Therein, it was stated that "Expansion of output will make it possible to carry forward our security programs with less strain on the economy" (ibid, p. 12). However, "a major obstacle to further expansion of production is the shortage of capacity in certain industries. It is not possible to expand capacity in all directions at once" (ibid). Thus,

> The growth in our productive power was not achieved without considerable inflation, partly because the measures for controlling inflation took time to enact and get into operation. But since these measures have been in full swing, we have continued to expand total output without inflation. (ibid, p. 11)

The Council report itself expanded upon the view of growth, and selective controls were the key to expansion together with giving priorities to certain crucial sectors of the economy. As the Council stated:

> The invasion of South Korea a year ago decisively altered the course of the United States economy. Until then, our major efforts since the end of World War II had been concentrated on expanding civilian production to meet the high post war level of demand swollen by the shortages built up during the war, and on maintaining a high level of employment. (ibid, p. 33)

However, after the Korean hostilities began:

> we were confronted with the need to chart a new path for the economy. If we were to avoid a new world war, or be ready for one if it came, the obligation became clear to build up our defensive strength at a much more rapid rate and help our allies build theirs. Only in this way could the free world make plain its resolve to resist aggression. (ibid)

The Council report then continued to point out that the Korean conflict had brought about increases in consumer purchases of many goods and in both consumers and producers stockpiling goods. This diversion of goods into consumer purchases and stockpiles was a threat to the needs of the increased military realities of war (ibid, p. 39). Thus:

> Immediately after the Korean outbreak, it became clear that one of our most important economic tasks was to expand production of essential goods. The President's Mid Year Economic Report in July, 1950 opened with these words, 'Recent international events make it more important now than ever before that we maintain and expand our strength on the home front. For the sinews of all our strength, everywhere in the world, are found in what we achieve here at home. We must make full use of our great productive resources, our ever improving industrial and scientific techniques, and our growing labor force. We must redirect a part of these resources to the task of resisting aggression.' (ibid, p. 38)

Output did rise. In June of 1950, the index was 199 as compared to 1935–9. In January of 1951, it had risen to 221, a rise of more than nine percent. However, real output began after the second quarter of 1950 to rise by only 4.5 percent (ibid, p. 38). There was, in January, 1951, the General Ceiling Price Regulation to suppress demand-pull inflation which was worldwide due to the war. Also, the Defense Production Act put on export controls; tax increases; an excess profits tax; credit controls on the purchase of new homes and consumer durables; an emphasis upon maximizing agricultural output; and voluntary pricing standards. The Federal Reserve increased the reserve rates (ibid, p. 41). But in vindication of the growth emphasis and the use of selective controls, as wartime production began to expand, inflation peaked after February of 1951 as consumer expenditures peaked and declined followed by some price declines (ibid). The inflation peaked due to the end of inflationary expectations due to increases in output which decreased consumer fears of shortages (which had developed previously during World War II) (ibid, p. 42), and due to a drop in demand even while such sectors as steel, aluminum, electric power were increasing output so as to end supply bottlenecks. The end of supply bottlenecks allowed expansion to occur elsewhere (ibid,). Thus, growth was still the emphasis, as the *Midyear Report* of 1951 indicated:

First, we must speedily build up and equip armed strength ... The second and equally important part of our two-fold task is to keep our economy strong by assuring an adequate flow of civilian goods, and to make it stronger for the great challenge now confronting us – and the even greater challenge which could arise – by expanding our total output and by adding even more to our industrial capacity or industrial potential. In addition, we need to help other free nations in further developing their industrial strength. (ibid, p. 50)

To promote a strong civilian economy, while at the same time building up our defenses, requires both the expansion of productive power and the maintenance of economic stability. These objectives are often mutually supporting. For example, increasing production by increasing the number of people at work, and the hours worked, makes it possible to meet the needs of the defense program with more goods remaining for civilian use. (ibid, p. 51)

The economy was, in fact, doing well. As World War II showed, from 1940 to 1944, real output had increased by 60 percent; industrial production had increased by 90 percent; and durable goods were up 150 percent (ibid, p. 53). However, Korean War expansion could not be done as easily as the World War II expansion. In the Korean expansion, military increases would need to be offset by cuts in non-military expenses, even if the economy grew at 5 percent or more (ibid, p. 67). As in the 1940–4 period, since 1950, inventories had risen at a record rate, although one-half of that rise was due to price increases. However, between January 1950 and 1951, total production had grown by 11 percent (ibid, p. 58) due to increased use of the labor force and increases in capacity. The Federal deficit was –.4 percent in 1950, but in the first half of 1951 it was a surplus +4.1 percent due to new federal receipts (ibid, pp. 203f). Thus, growth can be the key. However, even if growth was the key, another essential ingredient to continued prosperity was a system of priority programming. As the 1951 *Midyear Report* (ibid, pp. 97–8) stated, there are four keys to a program of economic growth in the Korean War period.

First of all, it involves the application of an economic strategy, which fits together insofar as feasible the various major parts of the national effort ... Second, the programming operation involves a continuing determination of how the major goals are to be reached. What part can be accomplished through expanding supplies? What part needs to be accomplished through reducing demand? In this respect, programming involves the constant testing of various economic policies and detailed actions in terms of the basic objectives which they are designed to achieve ... Third, programming involves scheduling and timing. Not only must the major goals be defined ... but in addition the relative speed at which these various major goals are to be attained must be borne in mind. Otherwise, vast and unnecessary dislocations in production and employment could be caused by cutting back on some things faster than others are increased ... Fourth, programming involves a reasonably complete and continuous synthesis of inventory at one central point of all important facts about the progress of the whole effort, so that those concerned with policy may have immediate access to what is happening as a guide to what needs to be done. Programming, in short, is nothing more nor less than the application of sound and tested business methods to the business of national defense, which is the biggest business that we are now undertaking, and by far the most vital.

There had been some notable economic successes during the Korean War years. The amount of total output absorbed by the security sector had risen from 6 percent in 1950 to a projected 20 percent in 1952. Nevertheless, it was estimated that the 10 percent increase in output could be followed by another 5 percent so as to aid both the military effort and the consumer (ibid, p. 99). Thus, the problem was how to increase output, not how to ration it. This was to be done by an expanding labor force and an expansion in the productive capacity in steel, aluminum, fuels, chemicals, energy and transportation. Specific aids to those needed increases in productive capacity would be long-term purchase contracts; tax amortization to achieve needed expansion; choices as to the type of investment needed; conservation; participation of small business; restraints on certain types of consumer, government, and business spending; regional development; aids to agricultural output; and the full utilization of a trained labor force (ibid, pp. 99–104).

If the above sounds like a policy of firm controls, it was not. It was instead a policy of growth, priorities, and incentives. The purpose was to maximize output, not to control production. The same concept was behind the policies to end inflation. Inflation was evident during the Korean conflict. It was due to private spending in excess of consumer production due to the priorities of the military effort; the spending for military goods without tax increases; private savings or borrowing going to purchase consumer goods; and the never-ending spiral of increases in income being due to past price increases. If so, the policy to end the inflation was to properly assess the sources of that inflation and aim the stabilization effort at those sources. This was not a reliance on the interest rate to deflate the entire economy, but a reliance on specific policies, including price policies, to target certain sectors of misbehavior:

> In shaping and adjusting the stabilization program, it is essential that these sources of inflationary pressure be comprehensively identified, and their relative importance properly assessed. Only by this means can we find the take-hold points for policies adequate and effective in a particular situation. (ibid, p. 122)

As 1952 dawned, the last full year of the Truman Administration and the Keyserling Council began. In previous years, even the war years, military output had risen significantly without undue strains upon the economy. Output had risen by 30 billion dollars in 1951 and prices to 330 billion dollars (CEA, 1952a, p. 2). Unemployment was at only 1.7 million persons (ibid,). The Presidential Address to Congress indicated these successes.

> This expansion of our economy has occurred because the American people have never lost their faith in progress. They have rejected the idea that we have reached, or will ever reach, the last frontiers of our growth. Businessmen, workers, and farmers have dared produce more and more, confident that we had the ingenuity and the imagination to utilize this increasing abundance. They have not been held back by the fear that we would get into a depression by not knowing how to make use of the blessing of full production and full employment. (ibid)

Since the outbreak of the war, investment was up, steel output had risen. farm equipment had risen and power sources had increased so that:

This growth in the productive sector of our economy indicates that neither the size of the military buildup, nor the high level of taxation enacted to finance that build-up, has repressed business investment initiative. Instead, the problem has been to hold the expansion down to non-inflationary proportions. (ibid, p. 6)

Furthermore,

When we look at the whole picture, we find that true economy embraces two equally important elements: The first is the avoidance of unnecessary outlays; but the second, and equally important, is the making of necessary outlays. A nation which spent its resources foolishly would dissipate its strength. But a nation which was too timid or miserly in applying its resources to urgent needs would fail to build up 'its strength'. (ibid, p. 13)

The Council, in its *Report to the President*, continued the observations made by the President to Congress. Both the concept of growth and priorities were reiterated, plus the belief that the whole economy must grow, not just parts of it. It was not a mere question of "guns" or "butter," but how, if possible, can an economy do both. Indeed, to the Council, the phrase "guns versus butter" is a deficient terminology. It is much too categorical in its assumption of a sharp line between the factors that are essential for security and those that are not. In a race which promises to be more a marathon than a sprint, good diets, health, shelter, education, recreation and the good morale that depends upon all of these, are essential for endurance in our national security effort. Striking a balance between our needs in these respects and the primary defense is a vital problem (ibid, p. 41).

The Council report also stated the encouraging news that helped to validate the Council program. It was true that consumer prices had risen 10.8 percent since mid-1950 and wholesale prices had risen by 13.4 percent. However, since the General Price Ceiling Regulation, consumer prices had risen by only 2.6 percent, and wholesale prices had declined by 2.9 percent and the index of primary commodities had dropped by 15.7 percent (ibid, p. 55). Thus, even though prices were higher than before the Korean War, those price increases were leveling off, except in housing where there were still shortages left over from World War II, the Depression, and the increased birth rate (ibid, p. 60). Thus, rent control was still seen as necessary.

In the Korean War period, wages were increased – 7 percent since November 1950 to $1.70 an hour by November, 1952 (Ibid, p. 61). As a result, the Wage Stabilization Board had frozen wages on January 26, 1951 and wage negotiations were underway concerning the level of future wage increases, especially as they related to the cost of living increase (ibid, p. 64). Corporate profits before taxes were the highest on record (ibid) and the consumption–income rates had declined to slightly over 91 percent, indicating a decrease in consumption (ibid, p. 73). This meant the beginning of a decrease in profits from an all-time high (ibid, p. 64). Projections were that the security expenditures for 1952 would have to increase by 20 billion dollars (ibid, p. 95) to 14 percent of total output (ibid, p. 96). Thus, the question of "guns versus butter" and the allocation and control of essential goods became a problem as military defense must have a priority in wartime. The Council stated that:

The central task in halting inflation is to bring supply and demand into balance at the prevailing price level. Whether an increase in output actually will tend to bring demand and supply into balance at the current price level depends upon a number of factors. (ibid, p. 103)

There was a need to increase munitions, but an increase in munitions alone may merely widen the gap between aggregate supply and aggregate demand. Thus, as stated in the quote above, "a number of factors" were involved. The gap might be closed partially by an increase in the efficiency of production. This would narrow the supply–demand gap by increasing output without increasing incomes proportionately to the rise in output. Or, on the other hand, increased output may be achieved by increased employment. This might add to more goods and more spending, but as some of the increased income from increased employment would be saved, such savings would help to alleviate inflationary pressures, if any. However, if higher employment raised per unit costs, the result might be cost-push inflation. Of course, increased investment would decrease costs. However, as investment was taking place, incomes would rise faster than output. This would be inflationary. As a result of the above factors and a fear of inflation, the Council recommended the utilization of more workers instead of the use of present workers at the higher overtime pay or new investment which may be inflationary (ibid, pp. 103–4; 106–7). This was possible as, excepting certain industries involving high skills where retraining would be necessary, there was not a general labor shortage (ibid, p. 105). An increase of 1.3 million workers needed for the increase in defense and other production was, in general, possible (ibid, p. 106). Thus, growth, not rationing, was the policy suggested by the Council. The Council finally surmised that if price or wage controls were eventually necessary, the previous increase in the amount of consumer goods from an emphasis upon growth would make these controls more palatable to the public (ibid, p. 104).

The *Midyear Report*, 1952, was not specific as to proposals as Congress was adjourned. The Council did stress the improvements in the economy from 1939 to 1952 (CEA, 1952b, p. 1). Investment was up, as the Council had hoped it would be, to 38 million dollars from 14 million dollars in 1939 (ibid, p. 2). The per capita income had risen 40 percent, even considering increased taxes and prices (ibid). Thus, consumption had risen significantly. In 1952, it was estimated that one million new homes were built and furnished with washing machines, refrigerators, radios, etc. (ibid, p. 5). There was inflation, but there still had been growth in *real* terms, so the overall standard of living was still increasing (ibid), despite the war effort. The reason for this increase in the living standard was the concentration upon the expansion of goods and services instead of rationing (ibid).

The Council was optimistic. Production capacity was sufficient for national defense without inflation if proper safeguards against inflation were followed. There was enough private and public demand to support business activity and employment if there were a decline in military expenses. The Korean cease fire talks which began in July of 1951 were finally showing some promise and the war ended on July 27, 1953. The Council indicated in its mid 1952 report that if military expenditures declined, the recessionary results would be minor because total military expenditures in the Korean conflict were a smaller proportion of total output than had been the case with World War II after which a recession had not occurred (ibid, p. 112). Nevertheless, the Council suggested the substitution of military expenditures for nonmilitary expenditures in order to utilize the increased productive capacity and to maintain high employment and prosperity (ibid, pp. 112–13). The Korean conflict had been fought by increasing output, not by rationing the consumer. The result was an increase in production capacity and an economic potential. South Korea was safe militarily and the US economy had grown into greater prosperity.

The last *Report* of the Council was sent to Congress in January, 1953. As the newly elected President, Dwight Eisenhower, was soon to be sworn in, the Council reported more of its past successes rather than the enumeration of specific programs. The report stated that in 1929, before the Depression, the output of all goods and services equaled 172 billion dollars. By 1952, that had risen to 345 billion dollars both measured in 1952 prices (CEA, 1953, p. 1). Industrial production had doubled and agriculture output had risen 50 percent (ibid). In 1929, there had been 48 million jobs. In 1952, there were 61 million jobs and the average work week had decreased from 48 hours to 40 hours (ibid). In 1929, the average income was slightly above $1,000 per capita; in 1952, it was $1,500 per capita, both in terms of 1952 prices (ibid, p. 4). There had been such developments as the Tennessee Valley Authority which invigorated the South and, in the West, the Columbia River Project. In 1929, there were 23 million autos compared to 44 million in 1951. In 1929, refrigerators were in 10 percent of the homes but by 1951, refrigerators were in 80 percent of the homes (ibid). Indeed, home ownership had increased from 48 percent to 55 percent from the end of World War II to 1950 (ibid).

The above indicated not only the success of the Truman Era, but also of the preceding Roosevelt Era, both important eras to Keyserling's career up to 1953. The Employment Act of 1946, which was suggested by Keyserling and supported by him, had meant that there was a refusal to accept depression and an attempt to set specific guidelines for economic policy. It recognized the essential fact that the private sector and the public sector were tied together and that the guidelines of public policy benefited both sectors (ibid, p. 12). To Keyserling and to the Council, full employment was the objective. However, full employment requires economic balance as mass output requires mass markets and the wages to support the mass markets through consumer demand in a private enterprise system. Thus, for continual full employment it behooves both the private sector and the public sector to plan ahead. Inflation, which had broken out after World War II and during the Korean conflict, had been offset by increasing output through growth, not upon a significant system of controls and rationing. All the lessons learned by the Council indicated that the interests of individual groups must be reconciled with the general interest (ibid, p. 8). With these comments, the Council had summarized its success and its philosophy – a philosophy born in the New Deal of Roosevelt and extended into the Fair Deal of Truman. With the Eisenhower election, an era had ended.

The Eisenhower comparison: a brief note

In a comparison of Truman and Eisenhower, Donald McCoy states that the Truman administration was an heir to the New Deal of Roosevelt (see Chapter 1, herein), whereas Eisenhower "was the heir to Hoover's New Day of trickle-down prosperity and revolutionary social actions ..." even though, in reality, "the Truman administration could not do without capital growth to finance its goals, any more than the Eisenhower administration could do away with earlier social reforms and still sustain stability" (McCoy, 1984, p. 180). The first substantial Report of the Council of Economic Advisers to President Eisenhower and the latter's report to Congress came in January, 1954. The Chairman of the Council was Arthur Burns, later to become Chairman of the Federal Reserve and, later still, Ambassador to the Federal Republic of Germany. Other members of the first Eisenhower Council were Neil H. Jacob and Walter W. Stewart. The new Council under Burns was a distinct break with the Keyserling's Council. The new Council believed in the free market of the competitive market system. The Keyserling Council had believed in that too, but the Keyserling Council realized that all markets were not competitive and that some adjustments took too long to adjust for economic and political stability.

The Eisenhower Council also had to deal with the fiscal results of the end of the Korean War. Despite the fact that the Keyserling Council avoided a recession immediately after World War II in 1949, the Eisenhower Council did not avoid a recession even though the Korean War expenditures had been relatively minor as compared to World War II expenditures.

The Presidential Address of President Eisenhower in January of 1954 stressed decreases in military spending and increased domestic spending. It also stressed progress and encouraged thrift. It mentioned a social health and security floor. It stressed a use of antitrust legislation to control monopoly. It asked for Presidential authority over mortgage rates and asked for tax modifications. It called for a "shelf' of public works to be used in a recession and a highway program which resulted in the Interstate Highway System. There was a cut in expenditures which resulted in a five billion dollar decrease in taxes (CEA, 1954, p. IV). However, as President Eisenhower indicated before Congress, a recession did develop. The Report stated that: "Employment in January, 1954, is somewhat lower than in January, 1953. There seems to be a connection between this fact and the fact that in January 1953, we were still fighting Korea and are not doing so today" (ibid, p. V).

However, in its reaction to the recession and to government in general, the Eisenhower address stressed a different philosophy than had the previous administrations and stated those differences quite clearly. As to the role of government:

Traditionally, our government has sought to create and maintain a democracy of opportunity in which individuals have the general freedom and the specific opportunities to work, to spend, to save, and to invest, and the incentive to pursue these opportunities to the fullest extent.

This concept of the role of government has not been made obsolete by the events of the last four decades. Two world wars and a world wide depression brought a continued broadening of the scope of governmental activities, but this fact does not justify the oft-made assumption that the range of Federal activities must continue to grow. (ibid, p. 4)

As to the role of government policy and open markets in economic adjustments:

> Open markets and effective competition are the means of channeling productive efforts towards social purposes in a private enterprise system. Markets must be kept free from restraints that discourage the innovator for the benefit of established firms or products. Open markets provide ladders of opportunity up which the newcomer can climb ... This role of competitive markets is as basic to the proper functioning of our economic order as the secret ballot is to our political democracy. Government has a vital responsibility in this area, immensely complicated by large aggregations of capital under single management and large organizations of labor ... (ibid, p. 5)

> But ... size alone does not preclude effective competition. Cases abound in which competition among large firms turning out similar products, seeking steadily to improve them or to reduce the cost of making them, has speeded technical progress and price reduction to the consumer. Government must nevertheless remain alert to the dangers of monopoly, and it must continue to challenge through anti-trust laws any outcropping of monopoly power. It must practice vigilance constantly to preserve and strengthen competition. (ibid, p. 7)

> A dynamic, urbanized economy poses numerous hazards for the individual. No longer is free land on the western frontier available to those who want to make a fresh start. The spread of private pension and insurance plans and social security programs in recent years has strengthened the forces of economic growth by helping to relieve individuals from the anxieties attached to sickness, accident, unemployment, and old age. A further strengthening of social insurance is highly desirable. Yet it must be kept in mind ... that the individual has a responsibility to provide, as far as he can, for his own security, and that the Government can make its greatest contribution to the welfare of individuals by fostering improvements in their productivity. (ibid, p. 7)

In order to allow the citizen to increase his or her welfare, there was an emphasis upon thrift:

> It is essential that economic policy give encouragement to thrift. There is no place for a fear of thrift in a dynamic economy. Perhaps no greater contribution can be made by Government to the encouragement of thrift, and thus to growth of the stock capital, than to provide assurance that a dollar saved today will not go to waste through inflation of prices tomorrow. (ibid, pp. 5f)

However,

> But savings will go to waste, from the viewpoint of society, unless they are transformed into productive investment. This means that the economy must have an efficient, competitive, financial system, capable of channeling funds – risk capital as well as borrowed funds – into those lines in which they appear likely to be most productive. (ibid, p. 6)

The above quotes are difficult to refute philosophically, if anyone really wants to refute them. They do, however, exemplify the differences between the Roosevelt–Truman ("liberal"?) philosophy and the Eisenhower ("conservative"?) philosophy. Both were dedicated to free markets, to competition, to democracy, and, one might add, to anti-communism, The difference was (is) that the Roosevelt–Truman Era believed that markets were not perfectly competitive and could not be remade into that image. They also believed that market adjustments took time and may involve wide fluctuations that were highly undesirable economically, socially, and politically, such as the Depression of the 1930s. Also, the Eisenhower message is one of "status quo," not of reform.

In terms of "conservative–liberal" debate, quite often the "conservative" accuses the "liberal" of being anti-business. This is erroneous. The Keyserling Council was actually very pro-business and Keyserling went out of his way to meet with business leaders on a regular basis in many cities. The "liberal" tradition believes that markets are not always competitive and that adjustments may take time or be too destabilizing, due in part to the non-competitive nature of many markets. The Eisenhower "conservative" philosophy recognized monopolies, but stressed anti-trust legislation to prevent them or to restrain them despite the strong argument that antitrust legislation either has not or cannot do the job of restoring competition. On the other hand, the Keyserling record and its emphasis upon growth from 1946 to 1953 does show that there were fewer economic downturns than in the subsequent years of 1953 to 1960. The contraction of 1953 was managed by the "shelf" of public works, the divestiture of rubber plants by the government, a stress on home ownership and social security, and a decrease in government expenditures to reduce taxes. The record questions as to whether or not these were enough.

The Council, 1946–53: an overview

The Council of Economic Advisers under the direction of Nourse did have some political problems within it. First, there was the problem as to whether or not the Council should stress growth rather than merely stabilizing the economy. Nourse was for stability (Gates, 1968, p. 109), Keyserling and Clark were for growth. Keyserling and Clark were to win as is evident by, at least, the policy statements made after mid-1950 and during the Korean War. It was Keyserling's belief in the Congress, "setting maximum purchasing power as an objective of National policy in the Employment Act ..." (CEA, 1947a, p. 1; Gates, 1968, p. 79) meant growth, not mere stability for the economy.

The second problem was whether or not the Council should be involved in politics and whether the chairman should testify before congressional committees. Chairman Nourse said, "no" on both issues. Keyserling believed that as an appointee of the President, he served him and that it was his responsibility to support the President and to testify before Congress on the President's program. If he should disagree with the President, he should tell him. If the disagreement were basic, the President's appointee should resign. The first solution to the problem was that Keyserling and Clark testified, and Nourse did not. Finally, as Nourse resigned, Keyserling's influence became more dominant.

A third problem arose in 1951–2 over a policy issue. That was "the Accord." The Federal Reserve had been maintaining the interest rate on Federal bonds at a low rate. This was to ensure a low rate of interest for the economy to spur investment and to keep the market for government bonds stable. In essence, the Federal Reserve stood ready to buy all Federal bonds at the current rate of interest if need be. Keyserling agreed with the policy on the grounds that it stimulated investment and kept interest rates low and, very importantly to Keyserling, it helped maximize long-term growth via investment in new output and capacity.

However, as inflation took place during the Korean War, there was pressure to end the policy of maintaining low interest rates on Federal bonds. One of the arguments was that anti-inflation policy needed higher interest rates. Another reason was that there was no interest rate check on the amount of bonds that the Federal government issued. All were bought at the same rate. If there were too many being sold, there would be no market check via higher interest rates which might also be anti-inflationary. The result was "the Accord" which indicated that the Federal Reserve would continue to buy Federal bonds to support fiscal policy, but not at constant interest rates. This gave the Federal Reserve more power over interest rates. As a result, interest rates have generally risen and have become an important anti-inflation policy device, but, as Keyserling would argue, high interest rates have, by restricting investments, become an anti-maximum growth device as well. Thus, the "Accord" to Keyserling was a mistake of the Truman Administration.

Keyserling desired to maximize growth and stressed that the maximization of total output depended upon the high purchasing power of the consumer. The Nourse Council stressed stability, not growth. After 1950, however, Nourse had resigned and Keyserling dominated the Council with the aid of Clark. Thus, as "pre-Korean defense policies began to emerge ... expansionary ideas began being accepted" (Gates, 1968, pp. 115f). The growth emphasis of Keyserling was to be supplanted in the Eisenhower Administration by an emphasis upon stability, not growth. During the Kennedy Administration "the philosophy of getting the economy moving again ..." re-concentrated upon economic growth, rather than mere stability as a major policy emphasis, especially after 1962 (ibid, pp. 116f). Thus, historically, the Council has shifted from an emphasis upon growth and stability to an emphasis upon only stability. The more "liberal" Presidents have generally stressed growth, while the more "conservative" Presidents have generally stressed stability. It can be argued that President Reagan, a "conservative," stressed growth, but such a stress was based upon lower taxes and market responses. Keyserling would have set more basic priorities to program the growth to the areas of greatest need.

It can be argued that the Council of Economic Advisers has become less important now than in the Keyserling Era. It can also be argued that the Council of Economic Advisers has become less active now than then. Keyserling agreed with both arguments. He often argued that the policy of appointing academic economists to the Council, rather than economic practitioners, was the cause of the Council's demise. Indeed, in the Tenth Anniversary Celebration of the Council (1956), Keyserling indicated that the Council should re-assert itself by:

> First, the Council should reinstate its earlier practice of project-ing, in quantitative terms, needed levels of employment, pro-duction, and purchasing power ... Second, the Council should set forth and evaluate the Federal Budget as an integral part of the Nation's Economic Budget. Third, the Council's projections should not be limited to our major components of gross national product, but in addition should state quantitatively our basic national priorities and appraise their relative economic cost and necessity. Fourth, the Council should make those projections on a long-term basis – five years or longer – recognizing that we cannot live safely today unless we look ahead. ... Fifth, the Council should realize that it is not primarily an economic research agency, nor a statistical refinement agency, nor an inter-preter of past trends, nor a pure forecasting agency. Drawing of course upon these resources and techniques, it is primarily an agency to help determine needs and evolve policies and programs. (Colm, 1956, p. 71)

Perhaps what Keyserling is saying is that the government, the biggest business of all, should plan its long-term goals as well as business is expected to do.

Appendix 1
A Personal Postscript

The issue between the "liberals" and "conservatives" is not the free market and a free society. Both agree on those essentials. The far-left of the "liberal" wing (if they can be called "liberals") and the far-right of the conservative wing (if they can be called "conservatives") may have little to agree on. The middle stream, the largest parts of both the "liberal" and "conservatives," are agreed on free enterprise and a free society. The difference is how well free markets work and whether or not the competitive structure does exist in many places. Also, there is the belief that all groups do not share equally, and thus must be helped – the unskilled, for example, are the last to be employed, if at all. Policies of support and of education are necessary for these groups if they are to share equitably in the goods of a free society and economy. The disagreement leads to differences in policy, but even these differences are not incompatible. There have been "liberal" Presidents who have not been liked by business, but that does not automatically mean that that President is anti-business. I may not like or agree with my neighbor, but that does not, or should not, mean that I think that neighbor is "against me." The same is true of the politics of rationality.

Appendix 2
Keyserling's Anti-inflationary Policy and Cost Curves: A Simplified Analysis

The concept of continued economic growth as an anti-inflationary tool as postulated generally by Keyserling has had its critics, especially amongst orthodox micro-economists. A basic reason for this criticism was the latter's concern with cost schedules. In micro-economic theory, the usual cost schedule (herein, for simplicity, for the sake of the lay-reader, the average cost schedule – AC) was considered to be "U" shaped or "saucer" shaped. This means that the average cost schedules are drawn sloping downward to the right (declining average costs) until a point of maximum efficiency and, then slope upwards to the right (increasing average costs) as shown below in Figures 3.1 and 3.2, respectively.

In micro-economic theory, the firm would tend to operate at the lowest point on its average cost schedule (as defined where the average costs per unit of output were lowest). If, for example, output costs were $10.00 and output were 100 units, average per unit costs would be $10.00/100, or 10 cents per unit of output. If, on the other hand, costs were $16.00 and output were 200 units, then $16.00/200 gives us average costs of 8 cents per unit output. Thus, as 8 cents is less than 10 cents, the former is more efficient per unit of output as seen by points C, D in the figures.

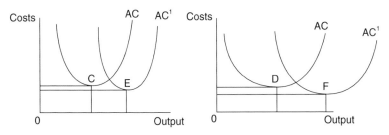

Figure 3.1   Figure 3.2

Beyond and to the right of points C or D, inflationary conditions begin due to rising average costs or of excess demand. As a policy to combat inflation, macro-economic policy would attempt to decrease demand and, thus output to the left of points C, D to decrease demand and the subsequent rise on prices (demand–pull inflation). To Keyserling, this could be counter-productive because (as discussed later in this volume) if a decrease in aggregate (macro) demand results in a decrease in output (supply), then the firm may be operating at a lower level of output to the left of points C or D. The problem is, to Keyserling, this new output is to the left of the level of lowest per unit costs on the A C schedules so that average costs are higher, as indicated by the A C schedules in the figures. Thus, as higher costs must be covered by higher prices if profits levels are to be continued, there will be an attempt to increase prices – which is inflationary – the very thing that the orthodox policy was supposed to prevent! Therefore, to Keyserling, this is an erroneous policy to combat inflation.

To Keyserling, an inflation is not primarily excess demand in relation to supply, but, rather, inadequate supply in relation to demand. Thus, to combat inflation, stimulate the growth of output (supply) rather than restrict it. However, this, too presents a problem as the micro-theorists (and others) point out. If, for example, cost schedules rise after points C, D (as microeconomic theory and the figures suggest), then the cost schedules (A C) begin to slope upwards and average costs rise, especially in figure 3.1 where average costs rise rapidly after point C, as indicated. Thus, firms will try to cover increased per unit costs beyond C, D by increasing prices, which is inflationary. Thus, to Keyserling, such a policy is wrong.

To Keyserling, the proper anti-inflationary policy is to attempt to stimulate output – supply to the left of points C, D; and, at the same time, stress technology and policy incentives towards technology to either (or both) shift the cost schedules to the right (A C^1) or shift them downwards.

If the A C schedules were shifted outwards via technology, more output could be produced at the same average cost. If the cost curves were shifted downwards, the same output could be produced at lower costs could as additional output as A C^1 would be below A C. This would tend to increase supply and/or decrease prices – an anti-inflationary result, as desired. In the figures, I have shifted the A C^1 schedules both to the right of the A C schedules and below them to indicate both effects mentioned above. This results in output at points E, F on the respective figures. In summary, to Keyserling, technology and policies to stimulate technological research and information are the most appropriate long-term solutions to inflation. The Keyserling keys are technology and the policy towards increasing technological development and innovation. We will return to this matter later in the text.

If the keys are technology, its adaptation and timing, a la Keyserling, what have been the results? In the nine-year period 1991–2000, the United States has had its longest period of post-World War II expansion. The economy has had high growth, low inflation, and low unemployment (high employment). In fact, unemployment was in April, 2000, the lowest in more than 25 years. Traditional economic theory (especially micro-theory) and such analysis as the Phillips' Curve (discussed later) would indicate that high growth and high employment would tend to be inflationary, but, as the above indicates, it has not been in the 1991–2000 period. The reason for this, as most economists including those at the Federal Reserve Bank agree, is that technology and cost-cutting by firms has allowed the economy to expand, employment to rise, and prices to remain relatively stable. Therefore, the Keyserling emphasis upon technology to combat inflation seems to be supported, both in the period 1946–1950 and 1991–2000; and, hopefully, 2000 onwards.

The analysis of the 1991–2000 period may actually mean (as speculated by some economists) that instead of the "U" shaped or "saucer shaped schedules 3.1, 3.2 respectively, we have a downward sloping average cost schedule even beyond points C, D (and E, F) given technology and increased efficiency, so that long-term average costs do not turn upwards beyond points C, D or E F (as from C E and D F). Such a prolonged scenario of decreasing costs is, to many economists, overly optimistic. In the long-run, short-run factors rarely remain constant. Nevertheless, technology, as in the 1991–2000 period, is an important key to the problem of combating inflation in the long-run. In subsequent chapters, we will return to technology and inflation, but in more general terms than in this Appendix. Also, the reader is referred to Keyserling's Conference on Economic Progress Pamphlets, especially 1959a, 1975.

4
Selected Testimonies: Hearings Before the Joint Economic Committee of Congress (HJEC)

Introduction

Keyserling testified many times before the Joint Economic Committee of Congress on economic matters. Each of his testimonies concentrated on the concept of growth: the concept of balance in the economy between the growth of output (investment) and the subsequent need for a growth of demand (consumption) necessary to absorb the increased output, and the policies which maintained these needed balances. Below, I will divide his testimony into two parts: the 1946–53 period of his membership on the Council of Economic Advisers, and the period after that time, 1953–87. The former period will be briefly covered due to its more complete coverage in chapter 3. Lastly, I will attempt to put the testimony in terms of an analytical perspective of what Keyserling was always attempting to say. This analytical framework will be expanded in chapter 7.

Keyserling's analytical perspective can be seen in his 1952 testimony on the *Economic Report of the President*, [US Congress: HJEC (hereafter HJEC), 1952] February 1, 1952, while he was still Chairman of the Council of Economic Advisers. The simplified example that he used was one of a triangle (ibid, p. 5). Figure 4.1 is my representation of that triangle as analyzed (but not constructed) by Keyserling. Superimposed upon it is a larger triangle which I have added to the original concept by Keyserling to emphasize his point more clearly in the long-run. I stress the point that the triangle is used as a *pedagogical* device only, and is *not* meant to represent any intensive analytical depth. Also, the relevant lengths of the respective sides of the triangle may and probably will change due to changing economic conditions, times, and policies. Also, of course, the triangle does not consider the foreign sector for the sake of simplicity and convenience to the reader. The more major parts of the economy (C, I, G) are, thus, emphasized by the triangle.

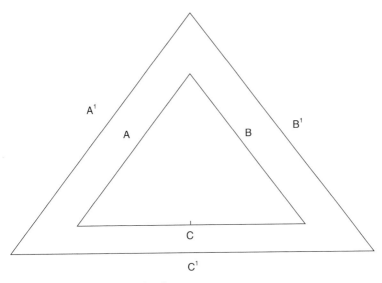

Figure 4.1 *The Keyserling triangle*

In the triangle, side A is consumption; side B is government outlays; and side C is investment in new capacity. The essential ingredient of a triangle is that all of the sides must connect, or else the triangle collapses. In terms of engineering, sides A, B, C have to be of specific lengths or else there is no triangle. In terms of economics that means that investment, consumption, and government must be in some proportion to one another. Investment on side C increases capacity. Consumption on side A consumes that capacity. The government on side B consumes what consumers do not plus carries out essential public expenditure that is not or cannot be done privately. As investment C increases, capacity–output, consumption and government must grow to absorb that capacity, the essential investment–consumption connection. As the economy grows via an increase in investment C^1, then the consumption A^1 and government B^1 must also grow. But the growth to A^1 and B^1 cannot be random. It must be enough to connect all sides of the triangle. If not, the growth in output C^1 cannot be absorbed completely by the growth in A^1, B^1. Overproduction will be the result. This leads to recession as supply C^1 exceeds ultimate demand A^1, B^1. Growth is necessary, but so is the balance between sectors of the economy – supply–demand. To Keyserling, this was an essential truism for both economic theory and public policy. It is, of course, true that the triangle may have a different shape given different conditions (in a recession, B or B^1 would be more important), but the essential point is that proportional growth between the sectors is necessary for full employment and full employment growth.

In the terms of economic policy, for example, Keyserling commented on the tax amortization bill to increase investment. To Keyserling, an increase in investment was good, but needed consumption should not be forgotten. Also, tax amortization would do more good if it were aimed at selected industries where the need was greatest. Lastly, he pointed out that necessary investment to increase output was not the cause of the early Korean War inflation. The cause was fear of scarcity or rationing which leads consumers to consume now, not later. This emphasized Keyserling's point that full production was not the prime cause of inflation if demand–supply balances are growing proportionally to one another. That is the simple, pedagogical message of the triangles.

The Council years, selected testimony

In 1949, Keyserling went before the Committee to state two facts. First, the Employment Act of 1946 was not anti-business. Instead, it was pro-business as policies to maintain economic prosperity meant business prosperity. The twin goals of stability and growth are beneficial to business (HJEC, 1949, p. 8).

Second, as the economy had been influenced by inflation, Keyserling indicated that inflation could be created by a rise in money supply faster than the rise in output. However, the solution was not necessarily to be found in decreasing the growth of the money supply since decreasing the rate of growth of money could also decrease the growth of employment and output. The essential anti-inflation policy was making certain that output, wages, and prices rose in relation to one another. If consumption exceeds output, one may need to decrease consumption, but one would also need to increase output – the balance in the economy (Ibid, pp. 27–8). This is especially true if some sectors of the economy have wages or prices going up faster than other sectors of the economy. Here policies should not restrict the entire economy, but rather, to control and expand the output of inflating sectors.

Price stability was no panacea to Keyserling. As he pointed out, periods of price stability had preceded major recessions in the past. Thus, anti-inflationary policies were not, a priori, a solution. The proportional growth of all sectors of the economic triangle was a better solution. Also, price decreases do not cause recessions. Instead, the cause of recession is prices remaining high too long ("overstaying the market"), especially if consumption has been lagging behind output without price decreases ("out-pricing the market") (ibid, p. 86). The policy should not be to cut production, but to expand it. If, as from 1939 to 1949, the cost of living had increased by 74 percent with a 29 percent increase since 1946 (ibid, p. 123) and farm prices had increased less than industrial prices, the problem was not too much output, but diminishing demand as real incomes fell and as disproportions between supply growth and demand growth widened. In 1929, for example, consumer expenditures were 76 percent of total output compared to 70 percent in 1948. On the other hand, investment had increased from ten percent of total output in 1939 to 15.4 percent in 1948. Balanced growth was the key to both the prevention of inflation and recession (ibid, p. 124). Consumption and investment must grow together if stability and full employment growth was to be maintained. However, in terms of national income, as investment was increasing from 10 percent in 1939 to 15.4 percent in 1948, the compensation of employees was dropping from 65.9 percent in 1939 to 61.5 percent in 1948 (ibid).

In 1951, Keyserling's testimony concentrated on the need for planning as an indication of the direction the economy needs to take. Just as traffic control – a form of planning – is needed in New

York, so is traffic control needed in industry (HJEC, 1951, p. 2). If there were a shortage of steel, one could argue for tax policies to increase the output of steel. However, the output of steel could go to use "x" or use "y" depending upon who can pay the highest price. If use "y" is more important or in shorter supply than "x", it may be desirable to give selective tax benefits to "y" use rather than to "x" use. Tax benefits to increase investments are fine, but they must point the increases in output in the right direction. When highway bridges are deteriorating, it makes sense to shift steel supply increases in that direction. It makes a difference whether the increased output for steel is used for more cars or for bridge repair. Cars are not too useful without safe bridges. Selectivity is sometimes needed – a problem of priorities (ibid, p. 2).

In the 1951 testimony, Keyserling pointed out a problem relating to wage–price freezes to fight inflation. To freeze wages in steel, for example, ignores the fact that steel workers do not buy steel. They buy housing and other outputs. To look at wages merely as a business cost ignores wages as a source of demand (ibid, p. 19). Thus, even though anti-inflationary policies may be necessary in the short run, balanced growth to prevent future inflation–recession is necessary in the long run. If specific shortages increase inflation in certain sectors, selective measures to stimulate growth in those sectors are needed. To Keyserling, it was the *lack* of growth, not growth, that was the problem in inflation. "Stabilization is essential ... but stabilization alone will not accomplish it. It is production which accomplishes it, allocation of supply. It is the setting of a higher target. It is programming and priorities" (ibid, pp. 273f). It is keeping the sides of those triangles in the necessary proportions to one another.

The post Council years, selected testimony

In 1955, Keyserling criticized the *Economic Report of the President* by commenting that its employment projections did not indicate whether that level of employment was too high, too low, or about right. The correct role of the Council of Economic Advisers is not merely to forecast, it is to guide toward maximum output, employment, and demand.

Some facts in 1955 disturbed Keyserling. Employment in 1954 was 1,000,000 lower than in 1953. The unemployment rate had increased from 2.5 percent to 5.0 percent, excluding part-time unemployment (HJEC, 1955, p. 163). As unemployment increased, consumers were hard pressed to maintain consumption. As a consequence, the savings rate changed from 7.8 percent (1952) and 8.6 percent (1953, p. iv) to a low of 7.2 percent (1954, p. iv). The last figure indicated that savings decreased as employment fell (ibid, p. 166). An increase in savings was a function of increasing growth, not declining employment–consumption of workers. As to growth, one needs more than growth; one needs goals (not mere forecasts) for increases in output, output mix, employment and income (ibid, p. 168).

In 1957, an anti-inflationary theme was developed by Keyserling's testimony. The problem of inflation in 1957 was one of some shortages and some surpluses, unlike the World War II period when there were mainly shortages. Economic growth had declined from 4.5 percent after World War II to 2.6 percent, 1953–7, to 2.5 percent in late 1956 (HJEC, 1957, p. 160).

The cause of the trouble to Keyserling was that investment, profits, dividends, and interest had increased faster than consumption. Thus, excess demand was not the cause of the inflation. Nor was it the lack of the savings of individuals, when corporations usually invest out of retained earnings, not the savings of individuals. The correct policy, then, was to expand output, not contract it (ibid, p. 160).

One method commonly called upon to fight inflation is a hard money policy which increases interest rates. This was, to Keyserling, a counterproductive policy (ibid). High interest rates limit plant investment, limit home building, and, thus, limit output and employment. Decreasing output increases inflation. To offset declines in output, firms increase prices to maintain revenues. So administered prices, not output shortages, are the problem of inflation. As during the Korean War, the correct policy was to increase output to prevent shortages and inflation. There may need to be selected policies to break bottlenecks, but that policy again stressed output increases, not decreases, to control inflation (ibid, pp. 164f). As the growth of real income had been less than 2 percent and the growth of consumption had been 2 percent (ibid, p. 166) and as investment grew by 10 percent, the output was not sustainable. Also, the Federal budget had fallen from 20 percent of Gross

National Product to 16 percent (ibid, p. 161). Thus, due to decreases in consumption and government, two sides of the triangle were decreasing; output levels fell. As a result, firms tried to maintain revenues by administered pricing. Also, to offset higher unit costs caused by lower output, administered prices tended to increase. Thus, a policy to cut the economy back further would increase inflation, not decrease it. The correct policy for balanced growth would be to concentrate upon growth: to return to the full employment budget concept developed by the Keyserling Council (and, later, by the Heller Council), to correct distortions in the economy, especially in regard to consumption, by means of maintaining real income, welfare, and the direct control of administered prices; to avoid hard money which hurts the weakest the most, and, lastly, to set targets for employment, output, purchasing power and priorities which the Council of Economic Advisers had previously done under President Truman (ibid, p. 168). As a brief point of departure, Keyserling also mentioned that most investment had been done out of profits and retained earnings. Thus, the consumer paid for the expansion via higher administered prices, and the corporations did not need to consider borrowing from outside sources. This helps to confirm Keyserling's belief in administered pricing (ibid, pp. 162, 166).

In 1962, Keyserling's stress was again on investment and the need for the other sides of the triangle to grow to sustain investment. However, by 1962, the economic performance had been dismal, despite an investment tax credit to increase investment and productivity. The reason for the failure to stimulate productivity was a slack economy (HJEC, 1962a, p. 566). Despite a tax credit, there was no reason to increase productivity if the economy was not growing at the full employment rate. Productivity is greater when growth is greater. They feed upon each other (ibid, p. 566), especially when real income demand is keeping up with increased output. If the labor force was growing at 1 percent and productivity was growing at 1.5 percent, growth should be at 2.5 percent. If there was excess capacity, however, that 2.5 percent will not be obtained. The maintenance of the system demands the balanced growth of the sub-sectors of the system (ibid, p. 580).

> if we want to aim for a much higher economic growth rate, we must intensify our efforts to get a higher growth rate in both

business investment and ultimate demand. But the statement that, to get a higher economic growth rate, we need a higher investment rate to GNP is clearly a *non sequiturs*. [sic] Such a policy would merely lead to more frequent recessions, and thus would average less investment and less productivity in the long run. (ibid, p. 582)

A tax credit might aid investment, but growth in investment is geared to output demand, not tax credits, *per se*. Also, investment tax credits should be selective so as to eliminate bottlenecks which limit the growth of other sectors of the economy.

In a later 1962 testimony (HJEC, 1962b), Keyserling maintained that we have underestimated the needed growth to maintain full employment. The reason was two-fold. One was the emphasis upon forecasting; the second was the lack of goals.

Forecasting and forecasting alone has two weaknesses. First, it forecasts. It does not guide toward or plan for the goal of full employment. Second, as it forecasts on past averages, it underestimates the full employment goal. Generally speaking, for example, if the real growth rate were 4.5 percent in year one, 3.5 percent in year two, and 3 percent in year three, then the average growth rate is 3.6 percent. To use the 3.6 percent growth rate as a policy guide ignores the fact that the economy has and could grow as fast as 4.5 percent. What is needed is a goal of 4.5 percent, the full employment goal, based upon a goal of employment, output, purchasing power, and selected priorities and the need for balance between the three sides of the triangle (ibid, pp. 252–4).

To Keyserling, both recessions and inflations were inefficient. All parts of the economy, including monetary policy and fiscal policy, are interrelated complements to one another. Economic inefficiency can be caused by an economy growing too slow or too fast – "just like a car going too fast or too slow burns too much gas per mile" (ibid, p. 254). Booms do not collapse because of insufficient profits or high taxes. Booms collapse despite low taxes and high profits. Businesses will not continue to expand if they see that they cannot continue to sell what they produce. Thus, even while profits are high, investment may fall (ibid, p. 292).

In 1963 (HJEC, 1963, Part II), Keyserling was supportive of the tax cuts suggested by the Kennedy–Johnson administration. However, to Keyserling, they were too small, too unfair to the poor, and over-looked the fact that increased expenditures are a more efficient way of increasing growth than are decreased taxes based upon their relative multipliers (ibid, pp. 701–3). The problem of growth, Keyserling re-emphasized, was inadequate income, maldistributed income and high profits that had remained despite the previous slack in economic activity. If investment plus productivity increases exceed real wage income increases, slow growth occurs because ultimate demand is decreasing relatively. To Keyserling, consumption was a function of real wages and investment was prolonged by the consumption of final demand. That is the message of his triangle analogy.

In 1965 (HJEC, 1965, Part III), Keyserling continued his analysis of tax cuts. Tax cuts could expand the economy, but eventually tax rates would equal zero (ibid, p. 99). Also, tax cuts could merely be saved, not invested; or invested in the wrong places (ibid). What happens then? There is a need for expenditures to stimulate the economy, not merely tax cuts. Also, as for the argument that low inventories mean equilibrium, Keyserling countered that low inventories might merely measure better management, not equilibrium (ibid, p. 97). The disequilibrium can be seen in the lack of balance in the economy and in the level of unused resources (ibid). In a critique of John Kenneth Galbraith's job-training suggestion, Keyserling retorted that job training presupposed that a job existed. To Keyserling, the best source of job training was a job. Jobs, of course, depended upon full employment growth. Jobs, plus the preservation of real wage income, were the two best anti-poverty programs. To Keyserling, "the jobs draw in the people, and they get trained mostly on the job, and in any even [sic] we do not know what to train them for until we know what jobs are opening up" (ibid, p. 99).

There were some other caveats of wisdom in the 1965 analysis. First, if farm parity payments equaled 58 percent of parity, this was farming subsidizing the public, not the other way around (ibid, p. 146). Second, overall wage guidelines of some set percentage for the entire economy were not good. As some industries have less productivity, and some have more productivity, an overall percentage subsidizes inefficient workers/industries and a high productivity industry would increase profits relative to the share of labor in those industries. The correct policy would be to set the wage policy for individual industries so as to benefit the most efficient industries and workers, not the least efficient. Lastly, overseas investment by Americans is a drain upon the domestic economy, but overseas investment by Americans is caused by inadequate growth at home, not by the chicanery of foreigners (ibid, p. 149).

In 1977, Keyserling again looked at the problem of tax concessions in his Congressional testimony. Tax credits, he maintained, do not create jobs if in the technologically advanced industries, technology is replacing jobs. Thus, the economic policy had to aim at job-training, the maintenance of consumer demand and government expenditures, all with the realization that by making jobs available, job-training will follow, not the reverse (HJEC, 1977, Part III, p. 425). The best job training was on-the-job training via a job (ibid).

In 1978, Keyserling appeared before the Subcommittee on International Economics. The economy had been slack and the strength of the dollar had been at stake. To Keyserling, the strength of the dollar was tied to the strength of the economy.

To Keyserling, the scenario that had threatened the dollar's value was in inadequate growth in the past. From 1953 to 1978, inadequate growth had meant that we had lost the equivalent of 5.9 trillion dollars in output and 75 million man-women-teenage jobs (HJEC, 1978, p. 70). From 1952 to 1978, high interest rates had transferred 1.5 trillion dollars from borrowers to lenders because of a monetary policy that was too tight. Keyserling indicated that Paul Samuelson now agreed with him that changes in the money supply must take into consideration the price level if we are to get an adequate increase in the money supply in order to maintain lower interest rates, economic growth and a diminished debt burden upon borrowers (ibid). The attention had been too much upon stable prices and too little upon increased output. After all, 1922–9 had stable prices, but 1929 saw the collapse. Stable prices, *per se*, are no panacea. The balance between consumption, investment, wages, prices, and profits is the key, not price stability itself.

To Keyserling, the economic policies leading up to 1978 were faulty. Long-term goals had been replaced by short-term responses to emergencies of the moment. Economic imbalances had developed that created inflation. The Federal Reserve had responded with tight money and, as a result, interest rates had risen, but the imbalances were not corrected, since there were no policies to point out and to decrease these imbalances. The first result was the greatest inflation since the Civil War and the greatest recession since the Great Depression. The second result was that the reduced output had led to more scarcities, increases in per unit costs, increases in administered prices, and inadequate productivity as increased productivity makes sense to introduce when the economy is growing, not when it is not (ibid, pp. 75–77). The problem of the weak dollar was, then, the problem of a weak economy. With little to invest in domestically and with increasing oil prices, the dollar went abroad. An emphasis upon balanced domestic growth was the solution, not further stagnation (ibid, pp. 83f).

In his testimony before the Joint Economic Committee in 1979 [HJEC, 1979], Keyserling looked upon the Carter Administration "with trepidation." The economic problems of the Carter years were many: inflation, a weak dollar, low growth, a rise in unemployment and a fall in output. An attempt to prevent further inflation, a Carter policy, Keyserling suggested, would decrease employment further. He reminded the Committee that in comparison to the slow growth during the Eisenhower years, the growth-orientated Kennedy-Johnson administration had reduced inflation to 1.5 percent and reduced unemployment from 7.6 percent to 3.8 percent (ibid, p. 50). In 1953, Keyserling reminded the Council there was a 2.9 percent level of unemployment and a 0.8 percent rate of inflation (ibid). As inflation was greater under the slack Eisenhower economy, inflation was a function of slackness, not of growth. Thus, an increase in investment and output coupled with an increase in consumption through real wage maintenance was the key; once again, growth is non-inflationary as long as it does not exceed full employment and has within it the correct balances between output, consumption and takes into consideration the needed priorities in areas of shortages.

In 1980, Keyserling once again criticized Carter before the Joint Economic Committee. As Keyserling predicted, inflation had increased beyond the President's prediction (HJEC, 1980, Part I, p. 206). Further, Carter had indicated that inflation would last until 1988 (ibid). To Keyserling, what Carter was saying was that the United States could not do as well as West Germany and Japan, both of whom had problems with increased oil prices. As Carter had suggested increasing unemployment to 6.2 percent in 1979, Keyserling saw this as a repudiation of economic growth for an acceptance of economic decline and a "deliberately projected" recession. A doctor, Keyserling retorted, is supposed to cure the patient, not to merely forecast death (ibid, p. 209).

By 1981, Keyserling turned his attention from the Carter administration to the Reagan proposals in his testimony of February, 1981. First, to Keyserling, the Reagan Administration was contradicting itself. The Treasury was talking about tax cuts without budget cuts. The Office of the Management was recommending budget cuts first. The Federal Reserve seemed to agree. The President was talking about both budget cuts and tax cuts (HJEC, 1981, p. 51). Keyserling reminded the Committee that to cut taxes to expand the economy and to cut the budget to contract the economy were counterproductive. The policy should be one of tax/expenditure to reach full employment, as had been attempted by the Keyserling and the Heller Councils. Also, he reminded the Committee that inflation was caused more by the high unit costs and administered prices of a slack economy, not an economy undergoing balanced growth.

Second, to Keyserling, there was no such thing as "supply-side" economics as contrasted to "demand-side" economics. There is only a "supply–demand" economy. The two sides of the growth equation must grow together. For balanced growth, the sides of the triangle must grow in relation to each other. If one increases supply by means of tax cuts, it made no a priori sense to decrease demand by means of budget cuts (ibid, pp. 52–3).

Third, Keyserling commented on the lack of savings that was supposedly (but was not) to be increased relatively by the tax cuts. To Keyserling, there were plenty of savings in retained earnings and elsewhere (ibid, p. 54). Indeed, a sluggish economy meant that savings must be in excess of current investment. What was needed was not an increase in savings, but an equilibrium of savings and investment at full employment. At full employment, there might not be a higher propensity to consume, but, due to growth, there would be a higher absolute level of saving. Consumers who are unemployed or consumers who see their real incomes decline cannot increase their savings. Savings, then, is a function of growth, not lower taxes. In the Reagan era, disposable income did rise, but real disposable income, adjusted for inflation, declined by nine percent. How, then, could consumers save?

The 1984 (HJEC, 1984) testimony before the Committee was a critique of the President, of Congress, and of economists. Keyserling pointed out the United States is no longer the leader in per capita income, in the rate of real economic growth, nor in the ability to help the poorest segments of the population (ibid, p. 62). The fault is the lack of planning and priorities for the long haul. The fault is looking at the problem of the moment or the economic theorem of the moment, while paying "little attention to the fact that it is production and distribution of goods and services that takes care of everything – everything – that we want and need economically" (ibid, p. 64). In the meantime, important priorities are neglected while we produce whatever we will. Keyserling finds many points of disagreement with the rhetoric of the Reagan era. First, anti-inflationary policy has forgotten long-term growth objectives (ibid, p. 65). Second, the deficit has grown in both recessions and recoveries. This means that it is no longer a "built-in stabilizer" for the economy. Also, the Federal deficit has grown and grown, as have the interest payment transfers to the holders of the debt (ibid, p. 67). Tax reductions have attempted to stimulate business and investment, but the regressive nature of the tax cuts hurts consumption. "Those 1981 tax cuts did nothing to stimulate business investment because they did not need funds; they needed markets" (ibid). Lastly, monetary policy has been too restrictive.

The restrictiveness of monetary policy can be looked at historically and in relation to its effect upon the economy in 1984. To Keyserling, ever since the Federal Reserve refused to support the interest rate on government bonds, (The "Accord" of 1951), interest rates had become variable and speculative. Also, the resultant high interest rates transferred income from the poor to the rich. Furthermore, the Federal deficits of the 1980s, despite their size, did not "crowd out" funds from private investment. Private investors had plenty of funds, retained earnings, and the ability to increase prices to enable them to increase investment by shifting interest costs on to the consumer (ibid, pp. 68–9). Thus, the deficit did not restrict investment, nor did Federal Reserve policy. If demand were there, investment would have increased. Thus, "crowding out" is not a problem. But even if "crowding out" were a problem, that is the fault not of government borrowing, but of Federal Reserve policy. The Federal Reserve can provide adequate funds whenever it wants to do so. The provision of these funds would lower interest rates, as occurred in 1933. Keyserling then indicated that Paul Volker's insistence that interest rates cannot be decreased until the deficit is decreased is *not true* and is *counterproductive*. It is not true because by providing funds, the Federal Reserve expands the free reserves, provides liquidity, and increases output [the author is reminded of the Federal Reserve's willingness to do so after the stock market crisis of October, 1987]. It is counterproductive because tight money restricts growth. The restricted growth generates fewer jobs, less output, fewer tax revenues and larger budget deficits. Thus, the Federal Reserve must share the blame for slow growth and cyclical developments. To Keyserling, Congress must have more influence over the Federal Reserve to make certain that monetary policy is pro-growth, not anti-growth; is pro-active, not retro-active (ibid, p. 68).

In 1985, the Subcommittee on Employment Opportunities (SCEO, 1985) of the Committee on Education and Labor of the House of Representatives held a hearing on "The Income and Jobs Action Act of 1985". Keyserling approved of the Act, but pointed out some problems in relation to a wider range of economic activity.

First, since 1953, the economy had been on a "roller coaster prosperity of ups and downs" with growth ranging from 5 percent (1947–53) to 2.1 percent (1979–84). The lower growth rates meant lost production, lost employment – the former estimated at 19.5 trillion dollars (1953–84, 1984 dollars) and the latter loss at 118 million years of potential production due to hours of excess unemployment, 1953–84 (ibid, p. 64). Furthermore, as the true level of unemployment must measure part time as well as full time unemployment, the true 1984 level of 7.3 percent was really 11 percent (ibid). As a result, the "gap between the house of have and the house of want…" has increased in recent years. This increasing gap, however, is not only a social problem, it is an economic problem (ibid, p. 65). Social inequality reduces consumption and, thus, limits potential investment and output.

Second, Federal deficits have increased, especially since 1980. The deficit, however, is not due to too much spending or low taxes. Rather, "the deficit … is due to the inability to squeeze adequate

Federal revenues out of the terrible and starved economy..." (ibid, p. 65).

Third, there is the increasing belief that Washington should let the States do much of policy innovation. But, Keyserling retorted, they never have. When Social Security was developed by Washington, only one State had it. Now all fifty have it. The Federal government has historically led; the States have historically followed (ibid, p. 68). In fact, this reliance on the States was one of Keyserling's criticisms of the Income and Jobs Action Act of 1985. Another criticism was that it shortened work hours to give employment to more people. Keyserling did not believe that "it can be successful to spread unemployment by giving less job opportunities to some in order to have some job opportunities for others..." (ibid, p. 68). The reason for this is:

> We do not just need to maintain the governing level of pay for fewer people, we need vastly to increase the total level of pay to all people, and that should be for fully employed people. The great trouble in the economy is ... a shortage of consumption, real wages of manufacturing now are lower than they were 10 years ago, while the fat have been fattened and the weak have been starved. (ibid)

In 1986, the Committee on Education and Labor (CEL, 1986) of the House of Representatives had an "oversight hearing" on the Full Employment and Balanced Growth Act of 1978 (1986). Before that committee, Keyserling stressed how well the Employment Act of 1946 had done in the periods 1946–53 and 1961–6 when full employment was the goal. In those years, it was recognized that "The great purposes of an economy are to wring from its naturally human resources the best that can be done in terms of production and full employment" (ibid, p. 6). But now, by 1986, a new theory, counter to full production, had taken over. As a result, the US lost $25 trillion of Gross National Product, or 106 million years of excessive unemployment and had "national economic deficits which are so much more important than the Federal deficit" (ibid, p. 12).

Among the theories that run counter to full employment is the theory that there is a "trade-off" between inflation and employment (the Phillips curve) despite the fact that the worst inflations have occurred when growth was slow. Another counter to full employment theory is the one wherein one has to balance the budget. Fortunately, Keyserling retorted, in 1939–45 the US did not say, "Well, it may be important to win the war, or to save us from destruction, but we cannot give that primacy over balancing the budget" (ibid, p. 7). Also, there is now the view that production, output, employment are the things to be measured, not such things as social, moral, or welfare aspects of economic policy. Social policy and economic policy, to Keyserling, are not separate, but interconnected. Social policies which help the poor help consumption, which helps investment, which increases output and employment and, furthermore, reduces absolute poverty. There is, thus, no dichotomy between social ends and economic growth. They are the same.

Another counter-theory to economic growth is the tax cut policies of the American political system. First, tax reductions are not as effective at stimulating growth as are expenditures. Second, expenditures can be more easily or effectively selective than tax selectivity, especially since an expenditure *is* an expenditure, but a tax cut may or may not result in the desired private expenditure reaction. Third, tax cuts have been regressive. Keyserling stated to the committee that "if I were in the top of the income structure, I got a 40 or 50 percent increase in my disposable income by the tax cuts; if I were at the bottom, I got a 5 percent increase" (ibid, p. 9). The result of all these regressive, counter to economic growth policies has meant that:

> Consumer income and spending have been adversely affected by regressive fiscal and monetary policies, by a hostile attitude towards those Federal budget outlays which help those first who need help most, and by failing to observe much less to remedy the decline in real wages and other sources of consumer spending. (ibid, p. 10)

The solution is to stress not balanced budgets and false Phillips Curve "trade-offs," but to stress growth, full employment and full production which history has proved to be not inflationary (ibid, pp. 8,11) – the message of both the Employment Acts of 1946 and of 1978.

Conclusion

In 1976, the Joint Economic Committee had a national conference celebrating the Thirtieth Anniversary of the Employment Act of 1946. Keyserling was not proud of the record of full employment under the act – not because full employment was unachievable (it had been achieved. 1946–53, 1961–6), but because no one was trying to accomplish it anymore. In his testimony concerning the Thirtieth Anniversary of the Council of Economic Advisors, Keyserling discussed eleven problems. In the concluding chapter, we will return to these eleven. Here, we will discuss the more analytically important ones for our current purpose.

The one problem that stood in the way of full employment was "wrong economic thinking, economic thinking based upon the economic textbooks instead of upon empirical observation..." (HJEC, 1976, Thirtieth Anniversary, p. 299).

Another problem that stood in the way of full employment was the erosion of the administrative quality of the Council; the lack of the Council attempting to set national goals and priorities; the substitution of active programs to increase employment for defeatist forecasts of unemployment; and a dependency upon the so-called immutable laws of economics; "instead of a stress upon the justifiable ... faith in our ability to shape our economy in accord with our potentials and needs" (ibid, p. 300). Instead of providing goals and priorities,

> Some of our economic advisors have been like a man driving up to an Exxon station and saying, "Fill 'er up." When asked whether to pour gas into the tires, air into the gas tank, and oil into the radiator, he replies: "What's the difference? Haven't you heard of Lord Keynes?" (ibid, p. 300)

Keynes, unlike that economist in the filling station, knew the difference, but many economists seemingly do not. Like putting air into the gas tank,

> We now hear that fiscal and monetary policies have failed, but they have failed only when misused. We need to improve and rely primarily on these powerful instruments. They do not

intrude on the government directly, or the private decisions, and that is good. (ibid, p. 301)

Another problem that has stood in the way of full employment theory is that monetary and fiscal policy have been ineffective. As the Exxon quote exemplifies, the failure of such policies has been in their misuse, not in their use. A fourth problem considered is any type of policy which forgets that economic stability depends upon not adversely affecting income distribution is destabilizing, not stabilizing. Furthermore, tax reductions and tax reforms are acceptable, but they are not a substitute for an expenditures policy, especially one that gives preference to needs other than solely private needs and stresses national priorities and public investments rather than temporary consumer fads. The point here is that the need for public mass transit may be greater than the consumer's need for more cigarettes (ibid).

Lastly, for our present purpose, is the myth that lower employment means less inflation. Time and time again, the opposite has been the case. But even if there were a trade-off between jobs and inflation, why value lower inflation more than jobs, especially when fewer jobs mean less potential growth for the nation and the people? The trade-off theory has allowed policy makers to promise less than could have been delivered. Thus, Keyserling throws at future policy makers a challenge:

No national administration on the domestic front has promised more than we could and should have delivered. Let us not now aspire to less; let us instead begin to match performance to promise. We have promises to keep. (ibid, p. 303)

But, as of now, our national policies have not yet fully aspired to fulfill all these promises. We are all the losers.

5
Keyserling after the Council of Economic Advisers: "The Conference on Economic Progress"

Introduction

After those years on the Council of Economic Advisers to the President, neither Leon Keyserling nor his wife, Mary Dublin Keyserling, retired. Neither one of them ever were the type of people to retire. There were too many things that needed to be done. One of the immediate projects of Leon Keyserling, as well as that of his wife, was the Conference on Economic Progress, which kept track of the economy; of economic policies; of the policies of the post-Truman Presidential Administrations; and proposed specific solutions to economic problems via the publications of the Conference on Economic Progress (CEP). There are too many such publications to deal with specifically here. However, the highlights of these in terms of the problems that Keyserling saw and the development of his thinking over the Post-Truman Era, 1953 to 1987, will be highlighted. They will show the development of both Keyserling and the economy of the nation from 1953–87. Keyserling's emphasis on growth, the role of low interest rates, the cost of high interest rates, and other social needs will be seen throughout. Herein, I will pick some of the "Conference Reports" that I believe to be the most important or relevant for today. Those selected will indicate the major economic analysis of Keyserling at the time in terms of the historic events of the time; his philosophy in relation to economic analysis and its purpose. Thus, herein, I start near the beginning, the Conference of Economic Progress Report of 1956.

A selected review: The Conference on Economic Progress

In 1956, Keyserling saw what he called *The Gaps in Our Prosperity* (1956) which had been caused by our "coasting along on the economic reforms and social gains built into the structure ... after the Great Depression" (Keyserling, 1956, p. 1).

> During the most recent years, the momentum of our economic growth has seriously slackened, and some new national policies have contributed to that slowdown. In consequence, total production and employment have been far too low for full prosperity. (ibid)

The "gaps" caused by the uneven prosperity of slow growth were seen in such problems as: (1) between 1953–6, interest income has increased 65 percent faster than wages; (2) dividend income had increased 75 percent faster than wages; (3) personal farm income had decreased 3.5 percent per year; (4) slums had been neglected; (5) resource development had been neglected; (6) education had been neglected; (7) health care, a key to continued labor productivity, had been neglected; and (8) US competitiveness with the Soviet challenge had been weakened as the US quality of life diminished (ibid, p. 2). In constantly attempting to balance the budget and in maintaining a hard money policy to constantly fight inflation, such important matters as national security, economic progress, and "human well-being" had been neglected and the hard-money policy to fight inflation had actually worsened inflation (ibid, pp. 4f). Keyserling quite often referred to "hard money" as the "upside-down fight against inflation" (ibid, p. 4). Orthodox economists would argue that "hard money" and high interest rates prevent inflation. To Keyserling, however, "hard money" raises interest rates to block investment which, to him, is not the means to increase output to fight inflation as discussed in Chapter 3, Appendix 2. Hard money via higher interest rates also benefits the wealthy, who own bonds, but not the poor who do not own bonds.

High interest rates also hurt the home buyer, especially the less affluent home buyers. Lower interest rates and the resultant increases in the growth of investment and productive output are a better and more equitable means of fighting inflation. Increasing output, not the "upside-down" theory of restricting output, is more likely to increase supply to close the gap between supply and demand. High interest rates not only decrease home buying but also decrease consumption of consumer durables related to home purchases. To Keyserling, high consumption was the motivation behind high prosperity and employment.

To end this "gap," Keyserling proposed a "National Prosperity Budget" (ibid). The goal was to increase employment, production, average incomes, minimum wage, small business aids, inaugurate balanced growth, and to improve the Employment Act of 1946 to encourage The Council of Economic Advisers to set concrete goals, not general philosophy. In regard to economic balance, Keyserling was certain that,

> Balanced growth in private investment and business incomes will be promoted, if consumer and public outlays are fully responsive to our needs and capabilities, if small business is encouraged, and if the proposed housing program is carried forward. (ibid, p. 7)

The keys here are a balance between consumption and investment. If there are investment shortages in some areas, priorities must be made to stimulate investment to fill those shortages. In addition, high consumption to stimulate demand and low interest rates to stimulate output are the keys to continued, non-inflationary growth. This growth in economy would balance the Federal budget by 1957. Such policies were, of course, both a continuation of his own policies under President Truman and a forerunner of the "full employment budget" thesis promulgated by Walter Heller during the Kennedy Administration after 1961–2.

To augment the above argument, Keyserling in 1957, turned back to a publication entitled, significantly, *Consumption – Key to Full Employment* (1957). Once again, Keyserling was concerned about the lack of growth in the economy. The growth rate of production had fallen from 4.5 percent per annum (1947–53) to 2.5 percent since that time and unemployment had increased by 40 percent since 1947–53

(Keyserling, 1957, p. 5). A major cause of the economic slowdown was due to the slowdown in consumption which accounted for 70 percent of the deficiency in total production (ibid, p. 12). The cause of the decreased consumption was "...deficiencies in wage income and depressed farm income" (ibid, p. 3). On the other hand, while consumption was decreasing from 1955–6, investment in producers durables had increased eight times faster than consumption (ibid). Obviously, supply was outdistancing demand. In addition, large numbers of persons were still in poverty – 68 percent of all were below a minimum standard of living income of $3,000 for a multiple person family and $2,000 for a single person family (ibid, p. 30). Consumption, the purpose of production, is also the leader in maintaining continued increase in production and economic growth. With inadequate incomes, consumers could not consume what could be produced. To Keyserling, full consumption required labor income to increase by 20 percent and depressed farm income by 72 percent to raise average family incomes to $7,600, an increase of $1,100 over 1956 (ibid, p. 1). This could be done by minimum wage protection, social security, old age assistance and welfare where needed. Also, the tax burden on the poor needed to be decreased; the farm program should use income parity instead of price parity (discussed later); anti-trust should be increased to end selected incidences of administered pricing and profiteering; and the hard money policy "costing consumers about 4 billion dollars a year to subsidize higher-interest recipients, should be abandoned" (ibid, p. 2). These policies would increase consumption plus reduce interest rates which would allow for more investment. Both continued and balanced growth on consumption and investment, via lower interest rates to aid consumers and producers, were the keys to continued economic growth. Continued economic growth means increased consumption, increased production and increased profits. The desirability of decreasing unemployment, a cause of low consumption, is vital for high consumption and high production for full employment and prosperity (ibid, p. 19).

Keyserling also argued that it is frequently believed that wages had outstripped productivity in 1956 and, thus, caused inflation. To Keyserling, however, wage rates had not risen faster than productivity (ibid, p. 20). Also, as the American economy had high unemployment, it also had excess capacity. Underutilized plant and equipment were not efficient. Thus, the argument that wage rates increases should have been held back because of the disease of faltering productivity mistakes the cause for the cure. Such a policy could lead to a downward spiral of the whole economy. If wage rates and consumption were higher, productivity would move upward towards its full potential (ibid) and cost per unit of output would decrease. Productivity is tied to full utilization and full utilization is driven by high consumption, not lower wages. Also, as the inflation was taking place only in a few sectors of the economy, a high interest rate policy retards the whole economy to decrease consumption and investment. A policy of selected controls over the inflationary sectors and low interest rates to stimulate investment and output increases (especially in the sectors where there are scarcities of needed priorities) makes, to Keyserling, more long-run economic sense (ibid, p. 42). My own analogy would be to ask, "Why use a shotgun that hits everybody when a rifle could have hit only the offender?" In the short-run, high interest rates affect everyone. Selective controls hit only the offenders. In the long-run, lower interest rates will stimulate the offenders to increase output, not increase prices. Thus, to end inflation through high interest rates not only hurts everyone, but also decreases the incentive to invest which then decreases output. An increase in output, not a decrease in output, is, to Keyserling, the long-run key to ending inflation.

The 1957 study on increasing consumption dealt with the farm sector only briefly. However, a 1958 policy statement, *Toward a New Farm Program*, (1958a), dealt specifically with the issue that has faced the American economy for over a century, from William Jennings Bryan to William Jefferson Clinton. The Keyserling report offered a Full Prosperity Budget for Agriculture which involved increased domestic and foreign consumption; farm production related to consumption; and farm income parity to other sectors of the economy (Keyserling, 1958a, p. 1). Since 1947, farmer's income (all sources) declined 23 percent in real terms while non-farm income had risen by 48 percent in real terms (ibid). The fatal flaw of agricultural policy, to Keyserling, was the assumption that: "organized protection of farm prices or income was the reason why farmers were 'producing too much;' that is 'overproduction' was depressing farm prices and incomes despite this 'expensive' protection" (ibid, p. 3). An often stated alternative was the laissez-faire solution of returning the farmer to the free market where supply would be adjusted to demand. However, to Keyserling, instead of that laissez-faire solution, the Employment Act of 1946 should be applied to the agricultural subsector of the economy (as well as other subsectors of the economy) to establish goals for maximum employment, production, and purchasing power (ibid, p. 4). The new approach concentrated on goals that "would merely substitute a voluntary but intelligently coordinated farm effort for a hodgepodge of errors, a prosperous agriculture for a depressed agriculture" (ibid, p. 6). The correct plan would concentrate upon (1) needed output; (2) the type of farm plant to produce the needed output; and (3) a higher farm income to provide the output and to provide decent farm living standards (ibid, p. 50). Keyserling, as the next paragraph indicates, realized that the laissez-faire policy was unfair to farmers, because, unlike the industrial sectors, farmers could control neither their farm prices nor their own incomes.

To Keyserling, the income effect was the major problem related to agricultural policy. As farmers could not control output and prices, due to the competitive nature of their industry, their market power did not allow them to control their incomes. Other sectors, however – big business, big labor – could control their outputs and, thus, their prices and incomes. To attempt to increase farm incomes, farmers produced more to further depress prices while less competitive industries reduced output to more successfully increase their prices and incomes (ibid, p. 41). Agriculture policy should not be to destroy competition, but to increase demand and adjust output to that demand. The next policy would be to subsidize the income of farmers not the price of agricultural goods. Such a policy would

> embody income goals for farm families, designed to reward appropriate production adjustments with a level of farm income and living standards moving gradually toward parity with that of the other Americans. (Keyserling, 1958b, p. 5)

In 1958, the study, *The "Recession" – Cause and Cure* (1958b), was published to analyze the 12 percent annual rate of decrease in production from 1957 (fourth quarter) to 1958 (first quarter) and the increase in unemployment to nearly 10 percent (Keyserling, 1958b, p. 1) which was a recession. A point stressed significantly by Keyserling was that both recessions and slow growth rates (1953–7) brought about an increasing differential between what output could be and what income was. Thus, if income had grown at the potentially possible 5 percent instead of the actual (1953–9) 2.3 percent, more production would have been possible. For example,

> under the high growth rate, in contrast with the low growth rate, the differential in total national production would be almost 400 billion dollars, and in man-years of employment, almost $16\frac{1}{2}$ million. (ibid, p. 3)

The anti-recessionary policy proposal cannot be laissez-faire because such a "let-things-alone" policy is too great a risk to take, because it is equally possible that a neglected recession could feed on itself and get worse. Thus, "let-things-alone" policy:

> fails completely to recognize that the immediate "recession" is part and parcel of a long-term retreat from full prosperity extending over many years. Merely terminating the "recession," without restoring full prosperity through a sufficient rate of economic growth, would be seriously short of our immediate need. (ibid, p. 5)

A recession or slow economic growth below economic potential decreases consumption, reduces potential taxes and, thus, potential public services and goods. In a recession, the output that is lost in one year cannot be made up in subsequent years (ibid, p. 12).

Instead of a "let-things-alone" policy, Keyserling suggested: (1) Federal assistance to states for payments to the unemployment of at least one-half of their previous wages to increase their welfare and their consumption of goods; (2) a tax reduction for low and middle income consumers, (3) an increase in budget fiscal outlays to stimulate output and employment; (4) a reversal of the "tight money," high interest rate policy combined with expanded outlays for low income housing to increase welfare, employment, and needed housing; (5) an increase of farm production, aiming at increased domestic and foreign consumption of agricultural goods, for farm production facilities and population to adjust to foreign and domestic needs, and allowing farm income to reach "parity" with other incomes; and (6) that some key industries should now make price reductions and wage increases geared to expanded consumption. The entire economy and the parts of it will (7) be able to do more when the Government assumes the prime responsibility to combat "recession" (ibid, pp. 3, 4). A full employment policy would solve both the problem of recession and the problem of inflation. That is a constant argument to Keyserling. The "gist" of the analysis is simple.

> The reasons are clear why stagnant and "recessionary" economic conditions breed far more price inflation than high level prosperity and a high rate of economic growth. The most important prices in our economy, with the exception of farm prices, are not determined primarily by laws of supply and demand ... and this is why they have come to be called 'administered prices.' These prices are set at a level deemed by businesses managers to be sufficient, not only to cover business costs, but also to yield what they deem an adequate level of profits. These profit levels in fact have frequently been much too high, and this means that the prices yielding these profits have been much too high. But regardless of whether profits have been too high, the tendency has been to attempt to compensate for an inadequate volume of production and sales by unusually sharp price increases during periods of low economic growth, stagnation, or even "recession." Under more satisfactory conditions of prosperity and economic growth, there has been more price moderation. (ibid, pp. 52, 53).

It is possible, of course, that this "price moderation" in expansion is due to the fact that the firm is operating on the lower part of the cost curve (as compared with a recession), per unit costs are less and, thus, price pressures are less. Full employment may breed both prosperity and stability. This is an essential point of Keyserling's analysis.

After a discussion of recession, Keyserling then turned his analysis to inflation in *Inflation – Cause and Cure* (1959a). The Eisenhower Administration had followed a "spurious crusade against inflation" that had restrained long-term growth, defense, and adequate health, housing and education of the public. In essence, to Keyserling,

> Restrictive monetary and budgetary policies, suited to wartime conditions when the economy was moving forward with such extraordinary rapidity as to exert tremendous inflationary pressures upon our productive resources, have been applied during recent years to slow down further an economy which was already moving too slowly and failing to make reasonably full use of manpower and plants. And going to slow, just as going too fast, is inflationary in the long run. (Keyserling, 1959a, pp. 1–2)

To Keyserling, the fiscal–monetary policies to restrict the economy (especially when the economy was already growing too slowly – 1.3 percent in real terms, 1953–8) (ibid, p. 2), – actually increased inflation. First, to restrict the economy after a growth of 1.3 percent was questionable. Second, and more important, the cause of inflation was being misunderstood. The 1959 inflation to Keyserling was not due to war nor to excessive spending or money supply increases, but, rather, after 1955,

> prices rose more rapidly as the rate of economic growth moved downwards toward stagnation levels and as chronic unemployment of plant and manpower increased. It was only the advent of an absolute recession that brought a temporary price stability, although even during the recession, some prices continued to rise. (ibid, p. 6)

The reasons for inflation in slack times are easy to determine. For example, "…an abnormally low rate of economic growth and a great slack in production resources sparked the new inflation of recent years" (ibid). Economic slack means that firms are not operating at maximum efficiency. Also, public housing and medical shortages, plus high interest rates, have put price burdens upon the consumer. Administered pricing in the food industry had also hurt consumers. Furthermore, industries that have administered prices have tended to "raise prices more rapidly as the rate of economic growth slowed down" (ibid). Thus, the new inflation was "due to deficient rather than excessive economic activity, and to shortages in public goods and services occasioned by deficient public outlays" (ibid, p. 7). Thus, policies to combat inflation should not be restrictive. Instead, inflation should be cured by (1) a rate of growth sufficient to use our resources, plants, and manpower more efficiently; (2) setting priorities to increase public and private goods in short supply; and (3) an emphasis upon income equity to balance production with the consumption necessary to buy that production (ibid).

The first step to counter inflation was the establishment under the Employment Act of 1946 of a "National Prosperity Program" of reasonable, quantitative goals for short-run maximum employment, production and purchasing power. Next, the government should stabilize the bond market at low rates of interest to make debt management less expensive and, if necessary, to use selective credit controls to pinpoint areas of specific inflation rates instead of the more general policy of higher interest rates. Such selective controls could limit luxuries as the expansion of necessities are aided by the lower interest rates. The same selectivity could be utilized in tax policies. Lastly, there should be some establishment of "broad criteria for prices and wages and profits, consistent with stable and optimum economic growth" (ibid, p. 8). Summarily speaking,

> In an environment of improved public policies, it would be much easier for the private sectors of our economy to establish the price-wage-profit and investment-consumption patterns which promote stable and optimum economic growth instead of boom, stagnation, and recession … [and would] … yield in the long-run far more price stability than the effort to "beat the business cycle" by price excesses when the weather is fair – and even when it begins to get cloudy. (ibid, p. 8)

It is important to note the emphasis upon economic growth, low interest rates, priorities, and price–wage–profit and consumption–investment patterns. To Keyserling, these factors were all tied together in the package of stability and high prosperity. The goals of price stability and growth are not contradictory. Instead, the two goals "interpenetrate, and when we forget either objective, we lose the other" (ibid, p. 9).

In a later study of the same year, *The Federal Budget, and "The General Welfare"* (1959b), Keyserling restates this view and discusses it in light of the need for increases in education, health care, the protection of senior citizens, protection of the unemployed and disabled, and public assistance. To pay for these benefits, "The Federal Government's revenues flowing from sufficiently rapid economic expansion would balance the Federal Budget before 1964, and maintain a surplus thereafter" (Keyserling, 1959b, p. 6). This, of course, was in line with the Full Employment Budget espoused by Walter Heller in the Kennedy Administration, but which Keyserling had been analyzing during his years on the Council of Economic Advisers. This idea is included in almost all of his subsequent Conference on Economic Progress Reports (1955, p. 13; 1959a, p. 57; 1957, p. 15; 1959b, p. 20, et cetera), the so-called "National Prosperity Budget" and its implications for micro- and macro- projections of needs and demands for full employment and high prosperity.

The costs of high interest rates were again analyzed in the Conference Report, *Tight Money and Rising Interest Rates* [Keyserling, 1960a]. To Keyserling, high interest rates limited investment growth, hurt the consumer, benefited the wealthy, and added to, not subtracted from, further inflation via increased costs (ibid, p. 1). Tight money was not a cure for the inflation disease, it was a cause. Again, to Keyserling, the inflation was not due to excess demand, but to selective price increases ("selected inflation") (Ibid). The correct policy was not to restrict the economy, but to expand the economy. The necessary tools would be the National Prosperity Budget; low interest rates to spur investment; the restoration of the Federal Reserve's ability to use selective controls; and callable features in government bonds if future interest rates should decline. Lastly, the 4.25 percent ceiling on long-term bonds should be maintained (ibid, p. 5).

An important part of the argument dealt with the view of the "conservatives" versus the "liberals." According to Keyserling, the "liberals" believe in economic abundance, economic stability, the protection of purchasing power, and human beings. Also, the "liberals" believe in "watering the tree at its roots" (ibid, p. 6). This can be compared to the conservatives who correctly abhor depressions, but believe that recessions help to "cure" the economy of excesses; and, in terms of income distribution, believe in "watering the economic tree at the top" (ibid) by benefiting wealthier groups who "save and invest." Thus, the "conservatives" neglect the "liberal" truism that "the production which results from investment must be sustained by consumption" (ibid, p. 7).

In terms of the money supply, the "liberal" believes that the money supply should be adjusted to change, but that monetary policy of the period 1953–60 had been too restrictive. The "conservatives," to Keyserling, support the restrictive money growth policies that slow economic growth, production and employment and redistribute incomes upward because conservatives are not "really convinced that a fully active economy is desirable; and, in distributing incomes upwards, via high interest rates, show a preference for 'watering the tree at the top' – the socalled 'trickle-down' theory" (ibid). To Keyserling, selective controls were a better way of controlling administered pricing-inflation rather than tight money as "tight money anywhere means tight money everywhere" (ibid, p. 8) and damages the whole economy rather than selectively controlling the inflationary sector. Thus, the price is paid by all – the public and the private sector – not by the guilty alone. Instead, under the Employment Act of 1946, a National Prosperity Budget would stress (1) investment to increase output supply; and (2) private and public consumption, including public works, to consume this increased output in terms of the twin goals of economic growth and price stability (ibid, p. 73). Once again, consumption is necessary to absorb output; and output is necessary for consumption at stable prices.

In 1960, a new recession began to emerge and Keyserling turned, once again, to the agricultural section in *Food and Freedom* (1960b). The essential message of this policy orientated study was the surplus in the farm sector and the lowering incomes of the farm sector. Keyserling pointed out that by 1959, farm income from all sources was 25 percent below that of 1947 in real terms whereas total personal income was up 54 percent in real terms (Keyserling, 1960b, p. 1). As a recession was beginning, Keyserling pointed out that diminishing farm income decreased the farmer's demand for consumer goods and for durable goods, including machinery (ibid, pp. 2, 67). The cause of farm income declines was not, to Keyserling, farm surpluses and, thus, lower prices, but rather, that:

Other groups, even with a large amount of unused productive power, can very substantially protect their prices and incomes by virtue of their strength in the market place. The farmer, even with a much smaller unused or wasted amount of productive power, cannot protect himself in the market place because of his relative weakness. (ibid, p. 68)

Following this then, the core of the problem is to improve farm income (ibid, p. 68).

The method of improving farm income was to increase the demand for agricultural products via feeding the domestic poor and the foreign people. The domestic surpluses should be used to feed those poor. However, a balanced farm program, a "Prosperity and Peace Budget for Agriculture" under the Employment Act of 1946. would set supply goals in terms of domestic needs, export needs, and adequate reserves. This would be to balance supply with demand with a reserve for future contingencies. In the meantime, the incomes of the family farm should increase to a parity with other incomes in the nation for the sake of equity and for the sake of increasing those families' consumption and investment. Keyserling, at this time, was rather vague as to whether this income increase should be in the form of price supports over needed products grown, or via direct income payments, as suggested by Secretary of Agriculture Charles Brannon in the Truman administration. This idea, stated simply, is the income goal for the individual farmer minus his or actual income from the marketing of his/her produce equals the direct payment to the farmer. This system supports farm incomes, not prices. Thus, the consumer benefits via lower prices; and the farmer benefits via higher incomes.

In the price-support system, agricultural prices are supported at a high level to protect the income of the farmer, but cost the consumer. In the income plan, agricultural prices are allowed to fall to the market level, and the farmer is directly paid the difference. The Keyserling proposal did recognize the presence and the results of differences in market power between sectors of the economy (competitive sectors and non-competitive sectors). The presence of the differences in market power is something either ignored by many economists or considered of no importance. This had led to mistaken policy based upon the assumption of a competitive market structure that does not, in reality, exist in all sectors of the economy. It should also be pointed out that agricultural production could not only feed the poor, it could also help to clothe them. In 1989, farm production could also propel the automobile by substituting fuels from agricultural products for the imported and polluting hydrocarbons presently in use. In the meantime, the problem of low farm incomes hurts the farmer, the consumer, the taxpayer, and diminishes the personal incomes of all via lost production and employment in industry since poor farmers cannot consume the output of the other sectors of the economy. As a result, production, employment, and prosperity, all keyed to consumption, grow slower.

The concept of growth was continued in Keyserling's *Jobs and Growth* (1961). Keyserling, once again, pointed out that growth and policies for growth were insufficient. In both "booms" and recessions, unemployment had been increasing. In the boom year of 1959, unemployment was 25 percent higher than the boom year 1955. In the recession year of 1961, first quarter, unemployment was 25 percent higher than the previous recession year, 1954. Thus, "we have suffered a long-range retreat from maximum production, with total output in the first quarter 1961 running about 15 percent below maximum production" (Keyserling, 1961, pp. 1f). Furthermore, both Congress and the Administration, had inadequate policies to bring both the growth rate of production and of consumption up to maximum. The Federal Budget in the fiscal year 1962 was to increase by only 3.5 billion dollars, or 16.5 percent of total national production in comparison to 17.1 percent in fiscal 1955 and 17.2 percent in fiscal 1959 (ibid, pp. 3–4). Thus, the growth in the budget was too small for maximum production and employment. On the other hand, the Administration had suggested a tax cut to business to stimulate investment in increased output. Keyserling opposed such a tax cut because it would stimulate an investment boom (as in 1955–7) which was not being absorbed by increased consumption on the expenditures side of the budget (ibid, p. 5). The essential problem of the Administration's policy was a lack of balance between consumption and production. A tax decrease policy would be desirable to increase output if consumption were also to increase,

But the current tax proposal seeks to stimulate business investment in producer facilities at a rate compatible with something like a 5 percent overall economic growth rate, while increasing public outlays and stimulating private consumption at rates compatible only with a very much lower overall growth rate. This repeats the errors of very recent years. Expansion in any sector will create some additional employment for a time; but when this aggravates instead of corrects distortions in the economy, we shall finally pay the piper. (ibid, p. 6).

The problem of balance was important to Keyserling but is overlooked by many policy makers. It was a dangerous oversight that led to fluctuations, not steady growth. Steady growth requires that consumption–production grow together at compatible rates.

As in the 1961 Conference Report (*Jobs and Growth*), and in his 1962 Conference Report (*Poverty and Deprivation in the United States*), the problems of unemployment and poverty were further analyzed. In the 1961 Report, it was pointed out that unemployment as a percentage of the civilian labor force had grown from 4.3 percent (1953) to 8.8 percent in 1961, including the fulltime equivalent of part-time unemployment (Keyserling, 1961, p. 9). The boom year of 1955 had a similar unemployment rate of 4.0 percent compared to the boom year, 1961, of 6.3 percent (ibid). The percentage of unemployment of more than 26 weeks in 1953 was 4.9 percent compared to 1960 of 11.5 percent (ibid, p. 10). Also, in many crucial industries the percentage of idle plant and capacity had increased from the 1954 average to the 1960 average: in steel, 19.1 percent to 48 percent; in electrical machinery, 16.3 percent to 26 percent; in chemicals, 18.3 percent to 23 percent; in autos and trucks, from 13.5 percent to 14 percent (ibid, p. 21). This represented a rise in the annual production deficiencies as a percent of maximum production from 0.4 percent in 1953 to 12.7 percent in 1960 (ibid, p. 22). Thus, actual growth had, since 1953, been below full employment growth. One of the reasons for the short-fall was that wages (demand) had not grown rapidly enough to buy the goods that would have been produced if higher demand had led to higher output. That is,

Especially during the "boom" periods since 1953 which led into "stagnation" and "recession," real wage increases as a factor in the expansion of consumption lagged far behind inducements (including price increases) to expansion of productive capacities. Further, even during periods of economic slack, the tendency of wages to hold their own or move upward in a "stabilizing" force, perhaps of more massive value than such "stabilizers" as unemployment insurance and automatic budget deficits. (ibid, p. 44)

In the 1962 Report (*Poverty and Deprivation* in the US), Keyserling concentrates the study on the 40 percent of the nation on low incomes. In 1960, for example, there were 10.4 percent of the families living on less than $4,000 per year (Keyserling, 1962, p. 24). Of all spending units with incomes of less than $5,000, 25 percent had no assets and 63 percent had less than $4,999 in assets (ibid, p. 28).

In 1960, President Kennedy had indicated that the top domestic issue was to prevent technology and automation from increasing long-term unemployment (ibid, p. 1). To Keyserling, that problem is "the same as that of maintaining a high enough rate of national economic growth to utilize fully the constant upsurge in our productive powers" (ibid). The failure to do so is because the US has not concentrated on overall goals to maximize production and has not concentrated on specific sectors where poverty and unemployment specifically are located, such as agriculture. Once again, it is a problem of goals, priorities, and balances between sectors of the economy, consumers and producers, not of automation *per se*. Realistic policy can make automation a blessing, not a "Frankenstein" (ibid). It is up to the American people.

The question arises as to whether or not there is a tax system that would help to reach these goals of maximum production and purchasing power. In *Taxes and the Public Interest* (1963) that issue was analyzed to promote growth of production and employment; to serve the national priorities; to advance social justice; and to balance the budget at maximum prosperity. The study supported President Kennedy's desire to increase the budget deficit so as to drive the economy toward full employment – the so-called Full Employment Budget concept pushed by Walter Heller of the Council of Economic Advisers. Keyserling pointed out the need for such a policy due to the unemployment rate of 5.9 percent (May, 1963), and economic projections of its further rise (Keyserling, 1963, p. 1). However, the tax cuts suggested by President Kennedy were, to Keyserling, insufficient because the resultant increase in disposable income would be too small to be effective enough to reach maximum production and purchasing power. Also the increases in disposable income would be unequally distributed – 2 percent for incomes less than $3,000 to 23.8 percent for incomes of $200,000. "This kind of distribution of tax reduction would work counter to a sustainable balance between investment and consumption, and is not justifiable in economic or social grounds" (ibid, p. 7).

To Keyserling, a more sufficient and equitable system of tax cuts would be cutting the flat 20 percent rate on the first $2,000 in taxable income to less than 15 percent; and establishing a minimum standard deduction of $400 for a taxpayer plus $200 for each dependent in addition to the current personal exemption of $600. Thus, a single taxpayer would have a tax-free income of $ 1,000 and a family of four a tax free income of $3,400 (ibid, p. 70). Other tax changes, corporate or otherwise, could be held back until later, if necessary. The tax decrease of ten billion dollars (with a multiplier of three) plus a proposed expenditures increase of three billion dollars (with a multiplier of 3.5) would stimulate domestic production by 40.5 billion dollars (ibid, p. 80). In addition, social security needed to be increased for the elderly; the minimum wage needed to be increased and expanded; and farm programs needed to help farm incomes–consumption. These programs, combined with the tax cuts, would drive the economy back toward full prosperity.

In 1964, Keyserling continued his stress on poverty and growth in the report *Progress or Poverty* which discussed the 34 million poor in the United States. Both of the Keyserlings continually stressed the problems of poverty and, once again, saw the question of poverty tied to the question of growth. In *Progress or Poverty*, 1964a, the related problems of growth and poverty were elucidated. However, the Report clearly separated the past from the present. In the introduction, Walter Ruether wrote:

> The time in human affairs when poverty was inescapable because the tools of production were inadequate to the eradication of this curse has now passed into history. We now have the science, technology, and economic capacity to abolish human poverty in our land. (Keyserling, 1964a, p. 1)

The proposals to progress were to decrease the taxes of the low-middle income groups and, more importantly, to increase expenditures, especially those directed at the poor. In addition, monetary policies since 1952 that had increased interest rates, which hurt consumers and investors, should be reversed (ibid, p. 137). There should be efforts to increase the consumption of the poor but, more importantly, employment increases should be aimed at areas where unskilled and semi-skilled are most employable. Thus, Keyserling suggested increasing housing and urban renewal and shifting housing funds from middle–high income housing to low–middle income housing (ibid, p. 138). Also, the minimum wage should be increased, and unemployment insurance should be both increased and expanded, along with the support of the elderly and, very important to all consumers, Medicare. Also, education and retraining to increase productivity and to shift skills from present to future needs must be expanded (ibid, p. 141). The government should also aid in solving problems caused by military or other government project dislocations by increasing aid to distressed areas, including those geographically distressed areas such as Appalachia (ibid, p. 143). Also, since persons could now travel from State to State easily, and, thus, effect unemployment levels and the cost of State services and poverty programs in those States, the Federal government should help the States provide those services. This would help to solve the problems of the migration of welfare recipients caused by what Governor Edmund Brown of California referred to in a *Harper's* magazine article in September, 1964, as "jet-age Federalism" (*Harper's*, Sept. 1964, p. 100; Keyserling, 1964a, p. 144).

The above calls for both planning and priorities. This, to Keyserling, was supportive of private enterprise, not antithetical to it:

> this suggested procedure would not improperly mingle private and public responsibilities, the general goals embodied in it would offer extremely useful information to the private sector of the economy. (ibid, p. 146)

as does indicative planning in western Europe. "It would help us to steer more effectively between the Scylla of doctrinaire statism and the Charybdis of doctrinaire laissez-faire. Nothing short of this can meet our own needs in the second half of the 20th century" (ibid).

Also, in 1964, Keyserling published a Conference Report, *The Toll of Rising Interest Rates* which he referred to on the cover as "the one great waste in the Federal Budget" (Keyserling, 1964b). This increase in the interest rates relates both to "spurious counter-cyclical monetary policy to fight inflation and to monetarism a la Milton Friedman to keep money growth rates constant. To Keyserling, it was always better to fight inflation via selective controls, especially when there was a large degree of administered pricing. Selective controls, combined with low overall interest rates to spur investment, would keep investment up in sectors where it was needed. To help control high interest rates caused by Federal Reserve policies, Keyserling suggested that the "independence" of the Federal Reserve be terminated. The Federal Reserve, of course, stresses the need to be independent from politics, especially in terms of economic policy. To Keyserling, this is spurious logic because

> The Federal Reserve spokesmen themselves have admitted the illogic of their position. For they have combined assertions of "independence" with exaggerated claims that monetary policy is a more powerful weapon for preventing inflation or promoting economic growth than almost any other policy. How can our national economic policies be fully responsible, if the one alleged to be the most powerful is allowed to proceed "independently." (ibid, pp. 82f)

At this point, Keyserling points out that western Europe central banks are not "independent," but have good records of monetary control. Keyserling, thus, suggests more congressional, more Presidential control, and the greater use of selective controls to reconstruct or to expand selected sectors as needed in terms of national priorities and employment needs. Thus, the Federal Reserve must "combine recourse to the aggregative approach with a much more selective and discriminating type of credit control" (ibid, p. 88). Furthermore, the fatal flaw in the aggregative approach of high interest rates is that it does not ration credit to real individual consumer or business or national needs. "There is no close connection under such a policy, between the ability to obtain credit and the need for it" (ibid, p. 88). Thus, a more discriminating type of monetary policy is a more pragmatic solution, especially in relation to needed priorities. Without selective controls, we risk feeding the fat sectors and starving the lean sectors (ibid).

One can see a partial argument in favor of less Federal Reserve independence in the Reagan Administration. The Reagan tax cuts and budget deficits (planned or unplanned) were for the purpose of expanding output – the supply-side argument. However, in face of the large Federal budget deficits and the fear of inflation therefrom, the Federal Reserve tightened the money supply which raised interest rates. The increase in interest rates restricted the supply side investment response to increase output. The slower economic growth diminished tax revenues necessary to close the deficit. The result was higher interest rates, slower economic-investment growth, a slower increase in tax revenues, and, as a result, a larger overall increase in the deficit. Thus, a tight money policy can act against "conservative" as well as "liberal" administrations. Higher interest payments on the public debt mean fewer public services elsewhere and transfer income from lower to upper income groups. It is a question both of economic growth and of economic equity.

In 1965, agriculture again returned as an interest. Keyserling called for a new farm program in the Conference Report, *Agriculture and the Public Interest*. The 1965 problem that Keyserling foresaw was that President Johnson had substituted supply restrictions for effective demand in terms of economic policy. That is,

> Instead of restricting "supply" because there is not enough effective "demand" … to use it fully for good purposes, we are acknowledging that "demand" can always be lifted to the levels required to use fully the productive powers which represent the core of our real wealth. (Keyserling, 1965, p. 1)

The problem is that this philosophy had yet to be applied to the farm sector. As a result, despite farm surpluses, farm incomes and farm populations were still declining to the point that the family farm was disappearing. Indeed, at least one-third of the unemployment was due to the number of workers forced out of agriculture (ibid, p. 25). The major problem was declining farm income. Not only was farm income declining, it was also mal-distributed. In 1963, 43.4 percent of all farm families had incomes below $3,000. In contrast, only 17 percent of the non-farm families were below

$3,000 (ibid, p. 8). Once again, low farm income limits farmers' ability to consume and invest and diminishes other sectors of the economy. Thus, decreasing farm prices and farm incomes is a mixed blessing, at best.

To Keyserling, inefficiency was not the cause of the farmers' problem. In fact, efficiency was rising rapidly from 81 in 1947 to 111 in 1964 with a base of 1957–9 = 100 (ibid, p. 33). Neither do surpluses cause low farm income because of this efficiency – over-production relative to demand. In terms of surplus stocks, in 1960 excess wheat stocks were equal to 1.5 years of consumption. In 1964, this surplus had been reduced to 13 months of reserves (ibid, p. 34). In 1964, wheat use was 115 percent of output. Tobacco use was 93 percent of output (ibid, p. 40). Thus, in wheat, there was need for more capacity, not less. From 1953–64, total farm output was only 1.8 percent over its domestic and foreign uses (ibid, p. 35). In 1964 only 0.6 percent of farm output was not consumed within the year. On the other hand idle plant capacity in steel was 24.8 percent and in automobiles 22.2 percent (ibid, p. 35). The real reason for the farmers' low income was not inefficiency or its opposite, over production, but, rather, it was the farmers' relative weakness in the market place (ibid, p. 42).

> the farmer buys in these highly organized and "administered" markets and sells in the "free" market. In consequence, even while a very small gap between what the farmer produces and what is used drives farm income sharply downward ... industrial producers are able to take care of themselves even when there is a huge gap between their ability to produce and what is used. (ibid, p. 42)

There should, of course, be an expansion in the domestic and foreign use of agricultural products, including fibers, by means of programs to aid the domestic and foreign poor. However, in condemning surpluses, we have never asked the supply question:

> What are the domestic needs of American consumers and industries for food and fiber output ... at maximum overall levels of employment, production, and purchasing power? Beyond meeting these needs, how much should our farm production capabilities contribute to the war against poverty ... What kind of farm

productive plant ... is required to meet these product-needs? (ibid, p. 81).

This is a question of goals and priorities in terms of need, both domestic and worldwide (ibid, p. 81).

However, the question of income parity is not solved by the above emphasis upon goals. Even when supply equals demand, farm incomes could still be low if farm prices were low in comparison to other prices. There must be a shift of emphasis from price parity to income parity. Keyserling pointed out that even during World War II when farmers had 100 percent price parity, they had only 60 percent or less income parity (ibid, p. 111). A mistaken emphasis upon price parity rather than income parity

> leads others to believe erroneously that the farmer is getting something very "high", and a form of "help" which others do not enjoy. A shift to the income concept would make it clear to all that the farmer is yearning only for what others *do* get: for example, through minimum wage legislation, but more importantly and abundantly through collective bargaining, and other practices prevalent in the non-farm sector. Thus, wage earners are able to increase wages, but the farmer has none of these advantages in controlling the income that they receive. (ibid, p. 111)

Thus, through a study of needs and a shift to income parity, both the problems of farm surpluses and low farm incomes could be solved. This would aid the rest of the economy by allowing the farmers to consume more and invest more to aid total production, employment, and purchasing power.

The crux of Keyserling's economic analysis and economic policy had always been the role of high consumption in maintaining high production, employment and prosperity. This was an essential point of *Progress or Poverty* (1964a). That emphasis was brought to the fore-front again in his first 1966 Conference Report, *The Role of Wages in a Great Society* (1966a). This was followed by a later report, *A "Freedom Budget" for All Americans* (1966b).

The problem of low wages and poverty, to Keyserling, was both a moral issue and an economic issue. The answer to the problem was the responsibility of both the public sector and the private sector

(Keyserling, 1966a, p. 2). However, one way of decreasing unemployment and poverty would be to increase the growth rate above 4.8 percent to a level equal to the full employment growth rate (ibid). The public's response to growth could be in defense spending and in the Great Society being carried out by President Johnson. Keyserling did acknowledge that, depending upon the times, increasing expenditures in both defense and Great Society Programs might not be possible without inflation:

> But if not, we could never in good conscience as a nation and a people choose to fight the war against the poverty which now oppresses more than 34 million Americans, in preference to restraining these satisfactions and luxuries even to a small degree which might be required. (ibid).

However, the expenditures to lift all the poor above the poverty level was estimated to be only 15 billion dollars or 2.2 percent of US total national product in 1965, or 75 percent of the tax reductions granted from 1962 to 1965 (ibid, p. 3). The Keyserling Report indicated that 60 percent of poverty was due to full or part-time unemployment or inadequate wages. By increasing the minimum wage from $1.25 an hour, a great deal of poverty could be alleviated. For example, a worker working 40 hours a week at $1.25 an hour still fell 20.1 percent below the poverty level of a multiple person family (ibid, p. 4). Legislation before Congress in 1965 to lift the minimum wage to $1.75 an hour by 1968 would help, but it should be continued up to $2.00 an hour after 1970 (ibid, pp. 4–5). This would put the worker 27.8 percent above poverty, but 33 percent below the "modest but adequate" level (ibid, p. 5). The cost to business in terms of total wages would be 1.5 percent. This is well below the 3.2 percent guidelines for wage-rate increases set by the Federal Price-Wage Guidelines (ibid). If there ever were a problem of total increases being outside the guidelines, the wage increases could be aimed at those with the lowest wages.

The concept raises the theoretical question of wage increases under the Federal Guidelines Act during the Viet Nam War. The specific US Act (as in Swedish policy in general) was designed to keep wage increases within productivity levels to prevent wages pushing up costs and, thus, prices. However, if a firm has low prices to consumers, should the low paid wage earners in that industry subsidize the consumer? A possible raise in prices to pay decent wages is not all bad. If the firm cannot raise its prices, perhaps income payments directly from the government to the workers is a solution based upon some above-parity income level for employed persons (ibid, pp. 6, 18–19) via direct payments to those receiving low wages, or a negative income tax arrangement. Of course, there is also the possibility that a firm that must pay substandard wages to sell its product should not endure anyway. The Swedes, who stress productivity, might agree. However, one possible solution briefly suggested by Keyserling, would be to give tax concessions to low wage industries. He indicated that there may be problems and objections to that policy, but indicated that we already give tax concessions to some very profitable firms paying high wages (ibid, p. 19). The point is that policy can be designed to be pragmatic.

The above stresses the moral aspect of low wages. Keyserling next turned to the economic effect of low wages upon the economy itself. Wages, as disposable income, are the basis of consumption, $C = f(Y)$. Consumption is the largest factor in total aggregate demand, so $Y = f(C)$ as high consumption generates high production which generates high national output and income (Y). The economic process is interconnected. Thus, the economy must maintain "the highest rate of economic growth feasible; ... growth must serve economic and social justice" and, "a sufficient portion of total production must serve the great priorities of our national needs" (ibid, p. 8, 9). The latter means that luxuries cannot replace necessities. Bluntly stated, a Rolls Royce is useless without a road to drive it on and an educated labor force to maintain both the car and the roads. Thus, there is an inseparable relationship between growth, social justice, and national needs. An economy must receive the funds to pay decent wages; to maintain a high consumption economy, to provide social justice; and to build and maintain the necessities of national life. All of these are obtained through the process of economic growth. The faster the growth, within feasible limits, the more easily the growing economy can provide the funds for all. Consumption demand is the powerhouse that generates the incentives to increase investment-production and, thus, the incomes for more consumption and further growth. To Keyserling, in 1966, "the deficiency in total wage payments ... quantitatively has become by

far the largest single element in the deficient overall economic performance" (ibid, p. 14). Keyserling goes on to point out the need for
increased consumption by pointing out that from 1953 to 1966 the
US economy had had more idle plant and capacity than at any time
since the Great Depression (ibid, p. 31). Thus, "there can be no
rational explanation of the idleness, except that our production
capabilities have been growing much more rapidly than ultimate
consumption" (ibid). So the need was there for the policies suggested by Keyserling. "The consumption lag reflects deficient consumer income" (ibid, p. 36) and, once again, "shortfalls in total
wage payments have been by far the largest single factor in the
development of excessive unemployment and inadequate economic growth..." as growth is tied to consumption and consumption to wages (ibid, p. 41). However, wages lagged even compared to production changes. For example, from 1957 to 1964,
productivity in the manufacturing sector increased 22.4 percent,
but wage and salary rate increased 16.3 percent. From 1961 to 1964,
productivity increased by only 12.2 percent, but wages and
salaries increased by only 7.7 percent (ibid, p. 47). Clearly con-
sumption/wages were lagging behind potential output. This was
to Keyserling, the "Achilles' Heel" of the American economy (ibid,
p. 8).

Following *The Role of Wages in a Great Society* (1966a), the
"Freedom Budget" for All Americans (1966b) was published which
contended that "this nation has the resources to abolish poverty,
for the first time in human history..." and that, "the very process of abolishing poverty will add enormously to our resources,
raising the living standards of Americans at all income levels"
(Keyserling, 1966b, p. iii). The point is that abolishing poverty
is not a cost transferring income from elsewhere, but an asset
generating future income everywhere. Poverty both reflects and
affects:

> the performance of our national economy, our rate of economic
> growth, our ability to produce and consume, the condition of our
> cities, the level of our social services *and needs* [my emphasis], the
> very quality of our lives. Materially as well as spiritually, a society
> affected by poverty deprives all of the citizens of security and
> well-being. (ibid, p. ii)

The principle of the "Freedom Budget" was to abolish want. The specific objectives were to restore full employment; to assure adequate income for the employed; to provide minimum adequate income for those who cannot work; to provide decent homes and to demolish slums; to provide all Americans with medical care; to conserve resources and the environment; and "to unite sustained full employment with sustained full production and high economic growth." Economic growth as a key to these objectives "not by robbing Peter to pay Paul, but under conditions which bring progress to all" (ibid, p. 3). The key here is production and the "economic growth dividend" from the Freedom Budget's emphasis upon economic and productive growth. After all, "we cannot enjoy what we do not produce" (ibid, p. 5). This was the challenge for 1966–75. Unfortunately, it has yet to be accomplished due to the lack of trying. Poverty could have been eliminated out of the "economic growth dividend," but it was never really attempted.

There is nothing theoretically new in the "Freedom Budget" and economic growth. It has been a part of economic analysis since and even before Adam Smith. All underdeveloped countries today are trying to increase their growth rates. Why? To increase the per capita incomes of the people. Keyserling was merely saying that an advanced country should have similar aims to those of underdeveloped countries – not to simply increase per capita incomes initially as an underdeveloped country hopes for, but to maintain that increase in per capita income to end poverty for all citizens and to allow those citizens to consume more of the products of increasing production. Consumption, from production, has been the heart of economic analysis from Adam Smith, through David Ricardo and John Maynard Keynes to the present day. Keyserling's contribution was to point out the essential connection for economic policy makers from wages, to consumption, to production and continued growth. That was an important contribution, but it is still too little recognized. "Freedom from want" is a moral issue. It is also an important economic issue that emphasizes the basic economic continued high prosperity. It is not peripheral to economic analysis and policy. It is basic.

The concept of high consumption was carried into the Conference Report, *Taxation of Whom and for What* (1969). To Keyserling, tax policy had four purposes: reconcile government expenditures to government revenues; encourage optimum growth; promote equity; and combat inflation (Keyserling, 1969, p. 1). Specifically, to Keyserling, the tax reform bills in front of Congress in 1969 missed most of these purposes. That tax proposal, to Keyserling, cut taxes too much; and the surtax was not justified on inflationary grounds or on grounds of equity because of its incidence upon lower income groups. If the tax reform was to reduce inflation, the tax reform should increase the taxes of the wealthy, not the poor, and, even if there were a problem of inflation, "the denial of tax justice, on the ground of fighting inflation, is part and parcel of entirely erroneous national economic policies which in fact have aggravated inflation" (ibid, p. 3). To Keyserling, inflation was caused not primarily by overheated demand, but by inadequate supply. The statistics point out the relevance of that observation. The period of 1955–8 was a period of recession, but also a period of high price increases. The period of 1960–6 was a period of growth where a decrease in unemployment from 5.6 percent in 1960 to 3.8 percent in 1966 was accompanied by price stability. From 1966–8, slower growth was accompanied by inflation (ibid, p. 4). The reasons for inflation accompanying slow growth are two-fold. First, the noncompetitive sectors of the economy where prices can be administered increase their prices in order to offset the losses from reduced sales due to declining growth. Second, firms producing below capacity are not utilizing their capacity efficiently as they are operating to the left of the point on their cost curves where per unit costs are lowest (ibid, pp. 4, 56–9). They raise their prices to offset the increase in per unit costs. Thus, recession can breed inflation. To have a fiscal or monetary policy which recesses the economy further, worsens the potential of inflation. An increase in output is needed, not a decrease, if inflation is to be ameliorated (ibid, p. 4). Thus, the tax cut proposed by Keyserling would be more toward the lower income classes for sound economics and equity; the elimination of the surtax as it was based on an erroneous view as to the cause of inflation; and the realization that decreasing taxes for the sake of decreasing taxes limits public expenditures, necessary public services, and economic infrastructure for continued economic growth (ibid). A tax policy to favor the poor consumer is "guided by the central principle that what is clearly best on grounds of equity and fairness is best for all by all other tests" (ibid, p. 61).

Once again, high consumption from adequate income is the basis of high production and general prosperity.

As high consumption and high production are tied together, so are *Wages, Prices and Profits*, the 1971 Conference Report. The report dealt with the policies to combat inflation from 1969 to the wage–price guidelines of August 1971 under the new Administration. These guidelines were, to Keyserling, more restrictive on labor wages than on business prices (Keyserling, 1971, pp. 3–4). The policies were based upon cost (wage) – push inflation. Keyserling pointed out that from 1960–6, real wage rates lagged behind productivity rates. From 1966–71, the real wage rates increased more rapidly than productivity due to idle capacity and economic slack, but that from 1970–1 (both third quarters), even though productivity gains were low, the increase in real wages lagged behind them. Thus, there is little cost–push argument for inflation (ibid, pp. 3–4). The result of the August, 1971, guidelines were more idle plant capacity, and more inflation (ibid, p. 1).

Before the wage–price guidelines – the "freeze" – Keyserling suggested that profits were too high to generate the investment capacity "required in ratio to ultimate demand," (ibid, p. 4). Thus, if current costs rise, because of the high profits, there is no necessary justification for the guidelines to allow for price increases. To Keyserling, the wage guidelines were too rigid; price guidelines were too lenient (ibid, p. 1). The correct policy would be to hold prices stable with some upward or downward adjustments where needed. If profits are too high, a tax policy could tax that away. If profits were too low, a tax policy or tax benefits could be instituted. Controls are not necessary. The worst and most self-defeating way to try to make profits "adequate" is to "budget real consumption and real wage incomes at levels below the requirements for full economic restoration," in an effort to "help" profits by restraining sales volume (ibid, p. 6). This is bad even for profits in the long run as profits in the long run depend upon demand and, thus, real incomes of consumers.

The major economic problem was the failure of the Nixon "freeze" to distinguish between goals and means. The goals are growth, social justice, and domestic priorities. These goals are inseparable as "the very programs and policies which would do the most to further priorities and justice would do most to underpin economic growth. The failure to recognize this has been, and still is, the crowning element in the prevalent confusion" (ibid. p. 11).

Growth, social justice, and selected priorities may be goals, but wages, prices and profits are not. The latter are means. Such terms as "fair wage," "proper price," or "reasonable profit" are meaningless

> except in so far as these concepts are derived from an analysis of what trend in wages, prices, and profits will combine (a) the economic balance between investment and consumption which is essential to optimal economic growth with (b) the distribution of the benefits which is essential to priorities and justice. (ibid)

Thus, in terms of the wages, prices, profits, it follows that (1) "The appropriate relationships vary greatly, depending upon the condition of the economy and the ultimate purposes in view" and (2)

> it is virtually impossible to try to delineate, and unwise in the extreme to try to enforce, standards or guidelines for wages, and prices and profits, without a short-range and long-range quantitative model of the economy as a whole, portraying the basic goals or purposes in light of our available and potential resources. We thus have more and more policies, but no unified policy; more and more plans, but no one coherent plan. (ibid, p. 12)

The failure to have a coherent plan in regard to imbalances between wages/profits or consumption/production is the problem behind economic instability. From 1953 to 1971, economic instability was caused by "boom" periods increasing investment faster than ultimate demand. The resultant excess production brought about a decrease in investment. The cause of the recessionary cut back in investment was:

> inadequate ultimate demand, and not from inadequate prices, profit margins, or total profits. These investment cutbacks, plus the more enduring deficiencies in ultimate demand, then led into periods of stagnation and recession ... Recovery movements commenced when ultimate demand grew sufficiently more rapidly

than investment to work down idle plant capacity, and thus to stimulate more investment on sound terms. (ibid, p. 23)

From the above, one may ask, "What is the correct wage policy?" Keyserling argues that the figures given by the Nixon Administration are the wrong figures. There were two figures used by the Nixon Administration, 3.0 percent and 5.5 percent (ibid, pp. 58–9). The 3.0 percent figure was based upon the average growth rate of long-run productivity. That rate of productivity (3 percent) includes periods of recession when there was little or no productivity increases. Because the 3 percent figure includes recessions, it (1) underestimates productivity increases by including abnormally slow growth periods; and (2) it has little to do with current growth rate figures. The 5.5 percent figure is equally wrong because it includes 2.5 percent cost of living adjustment on top of the erroneous 3 percent figure (ibid, p. 60). At this point, Keyserling seems to relate the needed productivity rate to the needed rate of increase in productive capacity. This might be done through indicative planning, but on this point Keyserling is unclear. Nevertheless, if the needed increase in productivity is 5.0 percent and if the cost of living adjustment of 2.5 percent is added, a 7.5 percent wage increase is to be allowed (ibid, p. 62). Despite such details, Keyserling generally adopted the basic framework of the Swedish plan. That plan suggests that if productivity increases were 5.0 percent, wage increases would be 5.0 percent. But, in this, another problem arises. The overall economy may have a productivity increase of 5.0 percent, but individual industries may have greater or lesser rates. Should the increase in wages be related to the overall rate or the specific rates in each industry? If they were related to the general rate, workers in good productivity industries, for example industry X, would receive wage increases less than their industry's productivity rate and workers in low productivity industries, for example industry Y, would receive wage increases above their productivity increases in their industry. The workers in the more productive industry X would be subsidizing the workers in less productive industry Y. Two solutions are possible. First, allow higher wage increases in industry X and lower ones in industry Y. That would mean that workers in industry Y were getting relatively poorer and that their consumption, the basis for high production, would lag. Thus, as a solution, a second suggestion is made. "The problem of

adequate wage rate advance (from the social viewpoint) in low productivity gain industries should be dealt with by appropriate minimum wage rate legislation, selective tax benefits, and other devices"
(ibid, p. 57). The tax benefits could be directed at the low-wage
worker as a subsidy to him or her. The tax breaks could be directed at
the low wage firm as a subsidy to it to raise wages or to increase productivity. It must be remembered that the problem of wages is related
to both social justice and to keeping the increases in production and
consumption in a ratio to maintain full employment growth. To
maintain full employment growth, consumption must expand
with output so that goods produced can be sold at cost covering
prices.

Keyserling turned his attention to housing in *The Coming Crisis in
Housing* (1972). However, to Keyserling, housing was both a social
issue and an issue related to labor employment, labor wages, and
thus, consumption and production. Keyserling had always been
interested and instrumental in the housing problem. It was always
obvious to him that the ghettos of our large cities presented a challenge to the economy to build decent housing for all. Indeed, 1971,
a high year in housing starts, was below the level of 1950
(Keyserling, 1972, p. 4). Housing construction meant employment
and employment meant consumption and consumption, through
the various multipliers, meant increased national income and
further production (ibid, p. 6). The 1972 Report on Housing recommended as part of the "Full Prosperity Budget" that there should be
developed long-run housing goals; that these goals be "designed to
promote sustained optimum growth" in the overall economy with a
recognition that attempting to decrease growth to control inflation
actually increased inflation; that taxes not be increased but made
more equitable and less regressive, especially the property tax
(whose diminishment may necessitate Federal revenue sharing with
local governments dependent on the property tax); that the money
supply increase should be geared to maintain low interest rates to
stimulate both increases in housing and productive investment;
and, lastly, that long-term Federal housing programs and targets be
initiated and maintained. All of the above would aid social justice,
employment, consumption and, thus, production and growth. In
essence, the growth of housing construction will help to maintain
the growth of the entire economy (ibid).

One could argue against Keyserling's growth theory that in the short-run at least, resources are scarce. This view was especially popular during the oil crisis and the stagnation in the 1970s. If it were true, Keyserling's proposals would have to be postponed. In answer to this restrictive philosophy, Keyserling put out the Conference Report, *The Scarcity School of Economics* (1973) with a subtitle, *The Shortages It Has Wrought*. Keyserling turns the main line of his attack upon the policy measures of the scarcity school. The policy measures of the scarcity school were to expand the economy in a recession, but contract it in an inflation. This type of policy, to Keyserling, was wrong, inequitable, and self-defeating. To him, the empirical evidence had shown that the anti-inflationary policies to restrict the economy have in fact augmented inflation (Keyserling, 1973, pp. 3, 28–31) via administered pricing; inefficient levels of production; high interest rate costs ("tight money") which must be paid for by borrowers; low increases in productivity in slack times; and uncertainty itself (ibid, p. 28). To make matters worse, as unemployment goes up due to the misguided anti-inflationary policies, many economists began to revise upwards the amount of unemployment the economy should tolerate in order to curb inflation (ibid, p. 31). This "natural rate of unemployment" hypothesis was an excuse for erroneous policy and an attempt to justify the high unemployment caused by the erroneous, restrictive, anti-inflationary policy. Instead, as before, the correct way out of scarcity is to allow a society to become more productive, not to restrict its productivity via repressive economic policy with its social consequences of higher unemployment.

But what about the 1970s energy crisis, *per se*? To Keyserling, the energy crisis was not caused by oil, but by US failure to increase other petroleum sources, including pipelines to transport the oil from other sources; and the failure to develop other forms of energy. One reason why other forms of domestic energy had not increased is that regulatory bodies allow a utility a rate of return on the capital actually used, not the amount needed for expansion in a growing nation. As a result, price increases in utilities have lagged behind price increases elsewhere. A proper attitude is needed. First, the rate of growth of utilities should be higher than the rate of growth of the overall economy due to substitution needs, technology, and increased industrial capacity. Second, it should be realized that a slow economy hides the real energy needs of a full employment economy. Thus, there is no reason to decrease utility construction in a recession due to lowering sales. "Rather, it is wise that the growth rate in utility investment, geared to long-range needs, should exert a 'counter cyclical' effect" (ibid, p. 63). The key term is "long-range." If the utility planners and the regulators had adopted the long-range view of future needs rather than the short-range view of present uses, the oil crisis of the 1970s would not have been an energy crisis.

As the stagnation of the 1970s continued, the Conference Reports came out with two policy statements for full employment, *Full Employment Without Inflation* (1975) and *Toward Full Employment Within Three Years* (1976).

The year 1975 was the worst recession since the Great Depression. Unemployment was over 7.1 percent by early 1975 and the deficiency gap between actual and potential output of 125 billion dollars (Keyserling, 1975, p. 1). In response, Keyserling stressed that the correct economic policies should be an expansion of the money supply by 8 to 10 percent for 1975, and into 1976 compared to 4.2 percent (1973–4) and an increase in fiscal expenditures. To Keyserling, a 40 billion dollar increase in fiscal expenditures would, given a multiplier of three, virtually close the deficiency gap, especially if there were a decrease in taxes for the low and middle income groups (ibid, p. 1). President Ford had suggested a more limited program of a one-year tax rebate of 16 billion dollars; an investment tax credit of four billion dollars (which Keyserling believed was unnecessary) and a policy to restrict the expansion of Federal programs topped off by a limit of 5 percent on cost of living adjustments (ibid, p. 2). To Keyserling, the tax rebate was inequitable as it gave up to $1,000 to rich and poor alike and the cost of living increase meant a reduction in real income levels. Also, the President's program was not only inequitable, it was insufficient (ibid). Lastly, the President's proposal to raise the oil import tax by 30 billion dollars would be inequitable to the poor and inflationary and, in a recession, damaging due to increased costs (ibid, p. 3).

In contrast, the Democrats in Congress had suggested a tax relief for the low/middle classes; a reduction in interest rates; public service employment, public works; housing; a review of the energy problem; and price surveillance, including some selective controls (ibid). They did not set quantitative goals, which to Keyserling was a serious oversight, but they were, to him, on the right track.

One reason for the conservative policies of the President was the so-called "trade-off" between inflation and unemployment, the Phillips Curve. This economic analysis indicates that the closer the economy is to full employment, the more rapid the inflation. The further from full employment, the less rapid is the inflation. This led many economists to justify high unemployment (rarely their own) for low inflation. The problems with the Phillips Curve are many. First, it assumes the conditions of one time exist for all times. Second, it assumes away reasonable policy responses (wage controls or guidelines, job training or productivity) as employment increases. Third, it ignores that statistical data suggest that if the Phillips Curve does indeed exist, it seems to shift a lot so as to be relatively unpredictable. Thus, to Keyserling, a policy based on the Phillips Curve was erroneous because the analysis was erroneous. Furthermore, if we followed the Phillips Curve and reduced employment, the economy would never reach full employment and full employment growth. If unemployment were allowed to remain too high, "...no one can be certain that the sensitive and volatile American economy could not break through the thin ice on which it is now skating, and plunge into a down-turn of depressionary rather than recessionary magnitude" (ibid, p. 4). The correct way to end an inflation would not be to restrict the economy (which Keyserling always noted actually increased inflation due to administered pricing and the less efficient levels of production), but to expand the economy giving priorities to the most needed sectors remembering, too, that for long-run stability consumption must keep pace with investment (ibid, pp. 19, 21).

To substantiate this argument, Keyserling pointed out that in the expansionary Kennedy-Johnson years (1961–9), the annual rate of real growth was 4.8 percent and unemployment declined to 3.5 percent from the inherited 6.7 percent. Prices rose by 2.6 percent, but price rises varied from 1.5 percent (1961–6) when growth was greatest to 5.4 percent when, in 1969, growth was the lowest. By contrast, during the Nixon–Ford years of slower growth (1969–74), the average rate of real growth was only 2.5 percent. Average unemployment increased to 5.1 percent and rose to 5.6 percent from the inherited rate of 3.5 percent. Price increases rose to 6.1 percent. From December 1973–4, growth rates became negative and unemployment rose to 7.1 percent and inflation rose to 12.2 percent (ibid, p. 23). This is, of course, a total reversal of the "trade-off' suggested by the Phillips Curve where price increases are supposed to decline as unemployment increases. Therefore, the correct policy to end upward price pressures is not to restrict output (which increases inflation) but to increase it, especially in priority areas where shortages and needs exist.

In conjunction with Keyserling's analysis, he presented a 16-point program. Briefly, the President should establish long-term quantitative goals to reach full-employment by 1976–7; shift essential or scarce resources to essential priorities; target selected shortages such as fuel, farm products, mass transit; increase public service employment; abandon the monetary policy of "tight money" and high interest rates; make tax cuts to the low/middle income groups; increase Federal expenditures, especially to needed priorities; balance the budget, but not until full employment is reached with tax increases on high incomes, if necessary, at that time; relate national defense spending to the international situation, not on an *ad hoc* basis; create income supports for the poor; build universal income supports to replace the myriad of "welfare programs;" gear farm output to needs to reduce the spread "between what the farmer gets and what the farmer pays," resulting from excessive margins in the distributive process (between farm prices and the grocery counter); eliminate the income and public service disparities between rural and non-rural areas; retrain workers for real jobs; anti-trust vigor; limit the growth of monopolistic tendencies; direct controls in selected areas of higher inflation; and, lastly, start domestic energy expansion over a wide front plus an emphasis on conservation (ibid, pp. 32–44).

The 1976 report continues the argument of the 1975 report. His line of reasoning started with the point that from 1947 to 1953 and 1961 to 1966, economic growth was high. However, generally, 1953 to 1975 had been a period of low growth and high unemployment. Between 1953 and 1975, there had been five economic cycles, and, as the growth rate was below potential, 3.3 trillion dollars of potential output and income (in 1975 dollars) had been lost. Finally, by December 1975, unemployment had risen to 11.2 percent and actual output was 250–300 billion dollars short of full production

(Keyserling, 1976, p. 1). This, to Keyserling, was hardly the intent of the Employment Act of 1946. What needed to be done was to: define the meaning of full employment; have the administration in power to aim toward full employment with long-range, selected, quantitative goals; recognize the government's leadership in closing the gap between potential and actual output through a coordination of public and private actions; set national priorities, economic and social; use fiscal policy to achieve the full employment goal; maintain decent living conditions, incomes, consumption for the disadvantaged; set forth standards for Federal Reserve action to maintain credit availability for these programs; abandon the idea that temporary price trends are of paramount importance and should not be used as an excuse to sacrifice long-term goals and policies. In relation to such temporary price trends, Keyserling stated, as discussed elsewhere in the chapter, that

> we should abandon the disastrous idea that price movements of themselves are as important as the real trends in employment and production, and the servicing of priority needs. And we should equally realize that the obsessionary act of fighting inflation by deliberately sacrificing these other objectives is the predominant explanation of the inflationary ravages which we have suffered for so long and endure today. (ibid, p. 5)

The policy solution to Keyserling for 1978 to 1980 was to set the growth rate to achieve full employment at 5.4 percent. Keyserling quipped that, "…'deep thinkers' who have made such a deplorable record of … attempting to restrain inflation to date" (ibid, p. 12) will say the rate of growth (5.4 percent) is too high. However, the Phillips-Curve-trade-off that they utilize is fallacious, and there is the need to make up for the lost production of 1971–77. Also, World War II proves that a growth rate as high as 9 percent could be achieved. What is needed is goals for future action – not more forecasts of current trends. These goals must recognize needed priorities and the selected policy means of achieving them (ibid, pp. 13f). If some sectors show signs of inflation, selective controls can be utilized. However, such problems of sectoral inflation should not be utilized as an excuse to not reach the goal of full employment (ibid, p. 5).

In the 1976 report, Keyserling attacked both of the then popular viewpoints concerning the Federal Reserve and Federal spending. In terms of the Federal Reserve, Keyserling pointed out that its "independence" could allow it to both counteract the policies of any Administration and to restrict the approach to full employment via "tight money" and high interest rates. According to Keyserling, no other central bank has that much independent power. The elected Administration, as the expressed will of the people, should, therefore, have more authority. Also, the Federal Reserve's money supply increases should be related to price increases, not to absolute values. For example, if price increases were 3 percent and if the money supply increase were 4 percent, that is only a real increase in the money supply of one percent and is, in essence, an extremely tight-money policy. But, to Keyserling,

> Support of an adequate rate of real economic growth requires that the rate of growth of the non-Federally held money supply be roughly equivalent *in real terms*. To do this, the money supply growth in current dollars must also allow for the general process of inflation. (ibid, p. 35)

That is, if the real rate of increase in the money supply were to be 5 percent and inflation were 3 percent, the actual rate of growth of the money supply should be 8 percent. One reason for this, of course, is that the high interest rates (resulting from a too slow a rate of real growth in the money supply) increase costs of borrowing to consumers, business, and government as well as restrict economic activity so as to widen the gap between *potential* and *actual* output. Full employment, then, cannot be reached and unemployment rises.

As to the American prejudice against government spending versus private spending, Keyserling was quite blunt in favor of the former, especially when necessary.

> Certainly, we want private enterprise to be encouraged to do as much as it can, toward developing a full and socially aware economy. But this cannot negate the proposition that, as Lincoln so wisely said, "it is the duty of government to do for the people what they cannot do so well or cannot do at all in their separate and individual capacities." Even the "inefficient" spending of

public funds to build schools and pay teachers is more econ-
omical in a true sense than the "efficient" use of private funds to
build gambling casinos at Las Vegas or luxury hotels in the
Caribbean. (ibid, p. 43)

If the Employment Act of 1946 expressed the views of Keyserling concerning economic policy, the Full Employment and Balanced Growth
Bill of 1977 (the Humphrey–Hawkins Act), actually enacted in 1978,
expressed Keyserling's view concerning growth, indicative planning,
and full employment even further. This Act (which has never been
fully implemented) adds to the Employment Act of 1946 by setting a
specific, quantitative goal of reducing unemployment to 3 percent;
sets a goal of reducing inflation, including remedies for selective shortages and priorities; recognizes that in dealing with aggregates, we must
also have "due regard to the balanced relation-ship among the component parts which are essential to success" (Keyserling, 1977, p. 2); sets
up the responsibility of the public sector to have not only an employment goal, but also energy goals, mass transit goals, housing goals, et
cetera; a goal for a balanced budget at full employment; a review of
monetary and fiscal policies, and a better coordination between the
President, the Congress and the Federal Reserve without creating
another agency (ibid, pp. 2–4).

The Act calls for more planning in the United States than is
normal. It is somewhat in line with French indicative planning.
However, it is not a planning act. The Act specifically states that it
disallows any attempts "to provide a government control of production or employment or allocations of resources, except to the extent
as authorized under other legislation" (ibid, p. 58). Instead, the Act
was an attempt to rationalize the myriad of government policies,
sometimes conflicting with one another; and to:

> blend these policies and programs into a unified program, instead
> of continuing a high degree of duplication and cross-purpose. It
> would reconcile short-range and long-range planning, in lieu of
> excessive emergency improvisation regarding the former and
> excessive neglect of the latter. (ibid)

Keyserling was always mystified as to why we would expect private
business to have short-term, long-term plans, but expect the

Table 5.1   *Summary of Keyserling's findings*

A	B	C	D	E	F
Periods	Average growth of nominal GNP (%)	Average growth of real GNP (1982) (%)	Inflation rate (%)	Unemployment rate (%)	Discomfort (%)
Liberal					
Truman, 1945–53	6.7	1.4 (3.0)	5.3 (3.7)	3.8	9.1 (7.5)
Kennedy/ Johnson, 1961–8	7.1	4.9	2.2	4.8	7.0
Average	6.9	3.15 (3.95)	3.75 (2.95)	4.3	8.05 (7.25)
Conservative					
Eisenhower, 1953–60	4.9	3.5	1.4	4.8	6.2
Nixon–Ford, 1969–76	9.05	2.65	6.4	5.8	12.2
Carter, 1976–80	11.2	3.1	8.1	6.5	14.6
Reagan, 1981–8	7.3	3.1	4.2	7.8	12.0
Average	8.1	3.087	5.0	6.2	11.2

government, the largest and most important business of all, not to have or even want to have such plans.

By 1979, it was becoming politically clear that there was to be a struggle between the "liberals" and the "conservatives." This was analyzed in *"Liberal" and "Conservative" National Economic Policies and Their Consequences, 1919–1979* (1979). The analysis therein approached the conflict on the basis of relative economic performances. The "Conservative" periods were 1919–33; 1953–61;

1969–79; and a mixture of mostly liberal (Walter Heller), but also conservative policies, 1961–9. The "liberal" periods were 1933–9; 1947–53; 1960–8. Which periods did better and what were the costs of the alternative program? Even though it is difficult to define "liberal" or "conservative," the periods suggested (1933–9; 1947–53 versus 1953–61 – i.e., Roosevelt and Truman versus Eisenhower) indicate the general meaning – generally non laissez-faire (liberal, 1933–9; 1947–53) versus laissez-faire (conservative, 1953–60), respectively, realizing that no one is really completely "laissez-faire." Also, the "liberal" would generally stress fiscal policy whereas the "conservative" would generally stress monetary policy.

From the myriad of data, it is difficult to generalize the results of Keyserling's findings for the present reader. In table 5.1, I will try to simplify and generalize on the 41 charts contained in his study, concentrating, where possible, on growth rates, unemployment, and inflation. I will further simplify by combining the data into Presidential Administrations where possible. Recognizing that each President has "liberal" ideas as well as "conservative" ideas (as do we all) and recognizing that there may be some differences of opinion as to who is "conservative" or "liberal," I have devised the simplified table 5.1. The general conclusions from it are in line with Keyserling's findings. Indeed, in his findings, Keyserling indicated that the "liberal" (pro-growth Presidents) had average growth rates of 5.8 percent (Truman, 1945–52); and 4.5 percent (Kennedy–Johnson, 1961–8). On the other hand, the conservative Presidents had growth rates of 2.6 percent (Eisenhower, 1952–60); 2.8 percent (Nixon–Ford, 1969–76), and 1.7 percent (Carter, 1977–9) (Keyserling, 1979, p. 61). Although my simplified methodology does not give those exact figures, they confirm that "liberal" eras have had better economic records than "conservative" eras of Presidential policies.

In an attempt to update the above, I went to the *Survey of Current Business*, Bureau of Economic Analysis Data and devised table 5.1.

In table 5.1, column A is the Presidential Administration defined as either "Liberal" or "Conservative," especially as those terms relate to "pro-growth" (liberal) or, "cyclical stability" (conservative). Column B indicates the growth in nominal Gross National Product (GNP). Column C, perhaps more meaningful than Column B, indicates the growth in GNP in real terms, that is, by taking into consideration price increases. Column D indicates the level of price changes (inflation) from year to year. The figure in parenthesis in the Truman years excludes the immediate post-war years of reconstruction when inflation was high because industry had not yet converted from war-time production to consumer-goods production even though consumers were demanding such consumer goods. Column E indicates the rate of unemployment. Column F can be considered a "Discomfort Index" combining inflation (Column D) and unemployment (Column E).

The reader will note several trends. In Column B, the nominal growth rates for the "conservatives" were usually higher than those of the "liberals". This is due to the inflation rate in Column D being normally higher for the "conservatives" than for the "liberals". When inflation is taken into consideration, as in Column C, the real rate of growth is higher for the "liberals" than the "conservatives." President Carter did, however, inherit an oil crisis from the Ford administration, which pushed prices up. In terms of unemployment, the "liberals" have a lower rate than the "conservatives", 4.3 percent as compared to 6.2 percent. In terms of the Discomfort Index, the "liberals" have an 8.0 (7.2 excluding the immediate post-World War II inflation due to the lag in post-war reconversion from military to consumer goods). By contrast, the conservatives have a higher Discomfort Index of 11.2.

The above seems to confirm the thesis of Keyserling that the economy has fared better under "liberals" than under "conservatives." To Keyserling, a "liberal" was one who stressed the continuation of economic growth. The emphasis would, thus, be on full employment output at all times. To Keyserling, a "conservative" would be one who stressed anti-inflationary policy to contract the economy in inflation which resulted in a "roller coaster" economy of ups and downs (ibid, pp. 57, 61). In fighting inflation, Keyserling stressed increased output (growth) whereas the "conservatives" stress decreased demand (contraction) which results in not achieving full employment growth.

Keyserling next analyzed the cost of the lost production from failure to reach full employment growth and to maintain that growth level, especially, as can be seen from the preceding data, during the conservative years. There is a large amount of data concerning the total loss of production due to actual output being less than potential output, 1953–9. Keyserling estimates that the lost production (the difference between actual and potential output) was over these years equal to seven trillion 1978 dollars (ibid, p. 62). For particular years, the difference between actual output and potential output increased from $6.5 billion (1947–53) to $540.4 billion (1971–79) (ibid, p. 103). These loss of output figures are, of course, only one of the economic statistics concerning the costs of "conservative" slow-growth policies that accompany the many other costs analyzed in the Keyserling Report, 1979. In terms of social costs, Keyserling indicates that in terms of the "conservative," low-growth policies:

There has also been reluctance to recognize that the man who is fishing in a clear stream running below beautiful mountains, because he is unemployed, is not really living in a good environment; that unsatisfactory schools, substandard housing, malfunctioning health care, and deteriorating cities are part of the environment in which we live no less than unpleasant smells or impure air in centers of industrial production. Well conceived optimum economic growth and environmental improvement are reconcilable and even complimentary objectives. (ibid, p. 57)

The attempt by Keyserling to correct the economic policies of the 1953 to 1979 period was expanded in 1980 with the publication of the Conference Report, *Money, Credit, and Interest Rates: Their Gross Mismanagement by the Federal Reserve System* (1980). This, of course, expanded on points that he had made previously. The period 1952 to 1979 is studied as a period of a too-tight monetary policy, which has resulted in high interest rates, decreased investment, production, income, and consumption. Since 1952, the average rate of economic growth has been far below its potential, meaning lost output, lost sales, unemployment, and poverty. There has been a continuing rise in idle capacity, which hurts business, workers, limits the potential income of consumers, and limits public revenues (Keyserling, 1980, p. 3). On top of this, the policies of the Federal Reserve have aggravated inflation, not ameliorated it.

The reasons that anti-inflationary policy that restricts growth and cuts back on output increases prices instead of decreasing, them are, to Keyserling, several. First, as demand falls due to the anti-inflationary policy, the firms that can administer their prices attempt to do so. As the firms' revenues decline, or as the firms' profit margins decline, the firms will attempt to raise prices to offset the revenue or profit margin declines. This is inflationary. Second, as the firms cut back output, they are operating to the left of the point of minimum per unit costs. Thus, costs per unit of output increase. To offset this, they will tend to increase prices. Third, as the anti-inflationary policy increases interest rates, the cost of borrowing increases. These costs will be or may be passed onto the consumer. Fourth, as higher interest rates decrease investment, this further restricts output and growth which puts more upward pressures on prices. Lastly, in the public sector, increases in interest rates also increase the costs of public borrowing for necessary expenses or for later stimulative policies. Thus, both the private sector and the public sector are losers.

To stress the points concerning the burden of higher interest rates, Keyserling looks at the ratio of total interest costs to GNP. These interest costs to GNP have risen from 5.2 percent in 1951 to 20.21 percent in 1979 (Keyserling, 1980, pp. 13, 17). The annual real economic growth rates also indicate a slowdown in growth as interest charges mount. The average rate of real economic growth 1953–79 was 3.3 percent compared to 4.8 percent from 1947–53, before the Federal Reserve's dominance after the "Accord" (ibid, p. 14) discussed earlier (Chapter 4, 1951–2). From 1961 to 1966, the growth rate that increased to 5.4 percent before the Viet Nam War seriously drained the economy after 1966. From 1969 to 1979, the annual real economic growth rate was 2.9 percent, and the last quarter of 1978 to the same in 1979 was 0.8 percent (ibid, pp. 14, 18). In the time period 1953 to 1979, the difference between actual output and potential output came to 7.7 trillion dollars (1979 dollars) based upon a conservative potential growth rate of 4.4 percent. The time lost in civilian unemployment was estimated as 80.5 million years more than if the economy had sustained nearly full employment growth (ibid, pp. 14, 19). Given this picture, what were the policy prescriptions for a revised Federal Reserve?

The policy prescriptions are aimed at the Federal Reserve itself. In the first place, Keyserling pointed out that earlier Presidents did not treat the Federal Reserve as "independent" as it is today. Its independence came in 1951 with the "Accord" which allowed the

Federal Reserve not to support Federal bond sales at current or low interest rates but, instead, to allow such bonds to "find their own level" (ibid, p. 100). This was the beginning of higher interest rates. This, Keyserling believed, was President Truman's gravest mistake. As a result, "Presidents have often preferred to suffer policies with which they have disagreed rather than to run the real or fancied 'political' risks of challenging the august monetary authorities," i.e., the Federal Reserve and its "independence" (ibid, p. 102). The monetary authorities are experts, of course, but Keyserling quotes President Woodrow Wilson, a founder of the Federal Reserve and a former President of Princeton University, who "once said that 'the expert always sees what is under the microscope under his eye, but never sees what is under his nose'" (ibid, pp. 103f).

To improve the quality of the Federal Reserve and its influence on the overall economy, Keyserling had some specific recommendations for the reform of the Federal Reserve. First, the *real* growth of the money supply should be legislated to increase by 4.0 percent a year, or higher, so as to achieve an increase in GNP of at least 4.5 percent per year. Second, the Congress should require that the Federal Reserve reduce interest rates by 50 percent, about two percentage points per year. Third, the Congress should require "universal reserve requirements" for banks and all financial institutions "to which Fed operations apply" and that no interest rates should be paid on these reserves. Fourth, under the Credit Control Act of 1969, the Federal Reserve should apply selective interest rate differentials on certain sectors of the economy. If a sector of the economy is expanding rapidly and bidding up prices of its inputs, higher interest rates might be necessary in that selected area. On the other hand, if an industry were finding it difficult to expand and if its expansion were seen as a needed priority, interest rates on that industry or sector might be kept lower. To Keyserling, this would aid in the meaningful establishment of economic goals and priorities (ibid, pp. 103–10). These reforms, among others, would stress to the Federal Reserve that it must consider not only what is occurring in the aggregate economy, but also what is happening in important sub-sectors of the economy. This is a point which Keyserling believes is important in forcing the Federal Reserve to maintain growth, not to restrict it in terms of short-run (and erroneous) anti-inflationary policies.

To Keyserling, a major fault with the Federal Reserve is that it is always leading in monetary aggregates and ignoring the amount of credit in particular markets. The insistence on a aggregative approach is a "blunderbuss" approach and "represents gross failure to take account of the relationships in the economy, the simultaneous need for more of some things and less of others, and the whole problem of economic balance" (ibid, p. 108).

In the above, four reforms of the Federal Reserve were indicated. These were mainly reforms related to the policy operations of the Federal Reserve. Keyserling did, however, suggest some reforms of the administrative structure of the Federal Reserve. First, the Federal Reserve should be more responsive to the elected President by cutting the Board of Governors term to 7 years and making the chairman's term coexist with the President's. Second, the members of the Federal Reserve board should represent all groups – business, labor, farmers, consumers, et cetera – not merely bankers. Lastly, the Open Market Committee should be made more representative. At the present time, the five members of the Open Market Committee that are drawn from banks often have only a banker's point of view. This means that under the present structure of the Federal Reserve, these five have a virtual veto power if they can get one or two of the members of the Federal Reserve Board to vote with them (ibid, pp. 106–8). Bankers, of course, like high interest rates because they lend, not borrow. This may involve a gigantic conflict of interest. Thus, the Open Market Committee should involve broader representation, including businessmen, consumers, farmers, et cetera.

The beginning of the Reagan Administration saw the beginning of the conservative era of "supply-side" economics with a desire to balance the budget from tax cuts that were said to generate increases in savings and, thus, investment. When this additional investment failed to materialize, budget deficits increased significantly. By 1989, the total Federal debt was 300 percent above what it had been in 1981 – almost 2.7 trillion dollars. Keyserling published the Conference Report, *How to Cut Unemployment to 4 Percent and End Inflation and Deficits by 1987* (1983).

The criticism of economic policy of 1953 to 1982 by Keyserling was based on deficient growth, the failure to grow at the US's full potential. The deficient growth from 1953 to 1982 was 13.3 trillion dollars of Gross National Product (1982 dollars) – four times the entire total national product of 1982 (Keyserling, 1983, p. 2). The largest loss was in 1969 to 1982, 11 trillion dollars (ibid). The period saw high unemployment and from 1953 to 1982, at the trough of each successive recession, unemployment rates increased and at the peak of each successive recovery, unemployment rates increased. In this way unemployment was growing both absolutely and relatively over the 1953 to 1982 period (ibid). Also, increases in the real rate of economic growth parallel increases in productivity. Thus, unproductively slower economic growth means forfeited productivity gains (ibid, p. 3). Fast growth seemingly forces productive use of productive resources or more innovations to increase the productivity of those resources and productive facilities. For example, from 1947 to 1953, real economic growth equaled 4.8 percent and productivity growth was 3.8 percent. In the period 1953 to 1960, as real economic growth declined to 2.5 percent, productivity declined to only 2.6 percent (ibid).

The period 1981–2 was referred to by Keyserling as the worst since the depression of the 1930s. He quotes a former member of the Council of Economic Advisers, Otto Eckstein, (*Time*, December 27, 1982, pp. 60–2) as saying, that the state of the American economy was worse than in almost 50 years (Keyserling, 1983, p. 8). A recovery would come, but Keyserling asked, what is a "true recovery"? The answer was that a "true recovery" was not changing from a –1.0 percent growth rate to a +1.0 percent growth rate. A true recovery to Keyserling was one that gets the economy back to what is needed to achieve "a reasonably full economic restoration" (ibid, p. 9). Also, the road to a true recovery is not mere economic forecasts or what is currently happening but, instead, the road to recovery involves

> forging dynamic and adequate policies *to make something better take place* [his emphasis]. The excessive substitution of forecasts or guesswork – which as so often turned out to be wrong – for dynamic and *probably aimed policy action* [my emphasis] has been a major affliction for a long time. (ibid)

But, Keyserling retorted once again quoting Eckstein, in which the latter indicated the hope for a recovery, but the fear that the government would do too little to bring it about (*Time*, December 23,

1982, pp. 60–2). What was Keyserling ready to do to achieve a "true recovery"?

The first policy Keyserling suggested was planning: especially long-term planning which at present was insignificant. Such planning would be under the aegis of the "Employment Act of 1946 and Full Employment and Balanced Growth Act of 1978" (Humphrey-Hawkins). Second, instead of paying undue attention to inflation and deficits, economic policy must concentrate instead upon growth which will solve both inflation and growth. Concentrating upon the former (inflationary deficits), not the latter (growth), is an example of "upside down priorities" (Keyserling, 1983, p. 14). Also, one must realize that deficits do not cause recessions. Instead, recessions cause deficits. Growth decreases deficits by increasing output, incomes, employment and revenues. Thus, the fiscal authorities must stress growth in order to end both inflation and deficits.

If the fiscal authorities should concentrate on growth. so should the Federal Reserve. For the Federal Reserve to tighten money and increase interest rates is, in and of itself, inflationary. This has previously been analyzed in this chapter. To Keyserling, the Federal Reserve's concentration upon restricting inflation limits long-term growth. For example, in 1983, Keyserling wrote

> In the yearning for economic recovery, the policy makers hail the recent reductions in interest rates. But these reductions have not gone far enough to help bring about a genuine recovery, and they are still very tight by historic tests. Furthermore, the policy makers among others have stated an awareness that, insofar as interest rates have been brought down somewhat by the severity of the recession, they will under "Fed" policies rise again as the economy really begins to recover. This, as in the past, will help to abort that recovery. The best example was the reduction in interest rates in 1980 during the recession preceding the last one, and the sharp rise to new heights when recovery started. (ibid, p. 15)

Keyserling then went on to stress that all sectors of the economy must grow together – the economic balance. As Keyserling stated

> If the ultimate demand created by private consumer spending plus public outlays fall far short of production capabilities caused

mainly by private investment, there is so-called "overproduction" which is really deficient ultimate demand. (ibid, p. 16)

Part of this "overproduction" is due to the lagging increase in wages, salaries, and farm incomes – it is the income of consumers which forms the basis of ultimate consumer demand. To exemplify his point, Keyserling indicated that non-agricultural average hourly earnings (1977 dollars) had decreased from an index of 100 in 1977 to 94.0 by the end of 1982, a decline of 6 percent, due to fewer working hours; and the decline in weekly non-agricultural earnings from $189.00 in 1977 to $167.65 in 1982, a decrease of 11.3 percent. The farm parity index ratio had declined 27 percent (ibid, p. 19). With this occurring to incomes, there cannot be an "adequate recovery based upon the needed amount of expansion of private consumer spending" (ibid).

There was then (1983), as now, much to do about saving more. It is said that increased savings are needed to increase investments. To Keyserling, however. low investment was not due to lack of funds. There are plenty of funds in retained earnings and earnings to lenders from high interest rates which borrowers had passed on to the consumer in the form of higher prices. Low investment is due to a bleak investment outlook, not the myth of inadequate savings. Indeed, the stock market boom is a sign that there are savings in the hands of the wealthy who, having an adequate amount of food, can afford to buy stocks rather than more food. More of these savings should be put into new investments, not merely into speculation of the stock markets. But increases in investment and output require increases in demand for the goods purchased.

There is also another set of problems that Keyserling foresaw. There has been a favoritism given to stimulus through tax decreases, not expenditure increases. Even worse, the tax decreases are not selective, so they have not been aimed at particular needs, priorities, and goals. They are tax cuts for the sake of tax cuts, not for the sake of helping to guide private funds to needed priorities. Of course, the easiest way to guide funds to needed priorities is expenditures, not tax cuts. The "neo-Federalism" of increasing State roles rather than Federal roles ignores the fact that the Federal role has always been important and has been of growing importance in increasing national economic growth and development. The States have contributed little historically to national growth (ibid, p. 23)

Lastly, the "trade-off" (Phillips' curve) myth is attacked, as before. The best record of low inflation has been during the highest level of economic growth, not the reverse as the "trade-off" theory implies. This, as we have pointed out previously, can be seen by the 1953 to 1982 data. To bring that up to date, in 1975 to 1976 the US had real economic growth of 6.2 percent and inflation of 3.9 percent. Later, 1978–80, when growth decreased to 0.7 percent, inflation increased to 12.6 percent (ibid, p. 21).

The fault of slow growth lies with us all. We have all accepted the theory of countercyclical economic policy at the expense of a long-term policy goal of maintaining high growth. But, to Keyserling, economists must bear a large measure of the blame.

> Our country could not have slid so far "down the greasy pole" if so much of the economics profession had not also slipped so far. The excessive use of fruitless econometric exercises, the timidity about evoking moral *criteria* and the tendency to "follow the leader" like a herd instead of asserting leadership, are all painfully obvious. Most of the "liberal" and "conservative" economists, whatever their political affiliations, have come closer together in aiding, or not opposing, the main lines of recent and current national economic policies. The trouble is not that economists are too much in disagreement; it is that they concur too easily. (ibid, pp. 24f)

With the criticism of economic policy, 1953 to 1981 what can be done policy-wise? Economists must reject the forecasting of cycles and begin the planning of long-term goals for full employment growth. An important part of this plan must be recognizing the role of public outlays. This involves a study of the total magnitude of the budget as well as the parts of the budget aimed at priorities. Thus, the Federal budget must also maintain consumption to maintain the needed balance between production and consumption. This balance for consumers involves social security, housing expenditures, food aid for the poor from "surpluses;" medical benefits, and other income–consumption orientated projects. Other needed expenditures are manpower training to allow the worker to maintain income and consumption while, simultaneously, training for the changing job structure and for an economy geared for full employment growth instead of one rolling along below full employment and full potential. These programs do, of course, involve expenditures. However, the expenditures generate the economic potential to generate revenues. A fully performing economy, as the full employment budget concept in all our introductory texts so amply verifies is the way to balance the budget – at full employment, not somewhere below it! But if growth is to be full employment growth, then too, the Federal Reserve must increase the money supply and keep interest rates low so as to not cut off the expansion. It must be remembered that decreasing growth actually increases inflation as business responds to increased interest costs and is forced to produce at less efficient levels by increasing their prices. Also, it must be understood that there is no conflict between government borrowing and private borrowing. The purpose of the Federal Reserve is to make sure that both private and public financial needs are covered. Government borrowing is one way of keeping the balance between consumption, public outlays, and production. The Federal Reserve cannot be allowed to ignore that crucial fact based upon some theory of "independence." As the economy is made up of flows and the continuation of these flows, the concept of the Federal Reserve's "independence" is ridiculous. All things are financed: consumption, public outlays and production itself. Thus, finance cannot be "independent." It is crucial to the continuation of all. It is crucial for both the planned priorities within the goal of full employment growth as well as the planned priorities with that goal. The goal involves both full employment plus the balance between the sectors of the economy needed to maintain it. We shall return to the subject in chapter 7 when we shall develop the analytical economic framework of the economic thinking of Leon Keyserling and its message to us today. However, we will end the chapter with the words of Keyserling which stress, once again, the need for growth, for priorities, and for long-term goals, not more short-term stabilization. As Keyserling wrote:

> In fact, stabilization is not the *primary* responsibility of the Budget, although it has a considerable significance. The primary responsibility of the Budget – as Lincoln said it best as to

government at large – is to *allocate a sufficient amount of total national product towards those purposes which represents what needs to be done and which others cannot do or do so well.* (ibid, p. 20; Keyserling's emphasis)

Thus, both the Federal Reserve and the Federal Budget are involved in the growth sustaining, prosperity sustaining, economic balance sustaining process for economic growth and equity – the purpose of Keyserling's analysis.

6
Other Writings of Leon H. Keyserling: The Problems of Economic Balance and the End of Poverty – the Crucial Connection

In previous chapters, we have examined the analysis of Keyserling from the Council of Economic Advisers (chapter 3); the hearings before the Joint Economic Committee of Congress (chapter 4); and the works of the Conference on Economic Progress (chapter 5). In this chapter, I will deal with his various *selected* writings in such places as the *New York Times*, *Challenge* magazine, *Harper's*, the *Atlantic Economic Journal*, and elsewhere.

The balanced economy and progress of poverty: the vital interdependence

In his early writings in the *New York Times* and his later writings in *Challenge* magazine, three vital parts of Keyserling's analysis can be seen and integrated. The first is that balance between the sectors of the economy is needed. The second is that economic progress or growth is an essential ingredient in ending poverty. The third is that the first two are intertwined with one another, not separate from one another. Thus, this chapter will specifically expand upon Keyserling's analysis by concentrating upon: (a) the need for balance between sectors of the economy; (b) the connection between growth and the end of poverty; and (c) the connection between the above.

In the fourth (1949) *Annual Report to the President*, of the Council of Economic Advisers, there was a section devoted to "Business and

Government," which stressed that economic policy was no longer to protect shippers of western grain from eastern speculators, or southern farmers from eastern bankers, a problem of the late 1800s to the 1920s. Instead, current policy should now concentrate primarily "upon the basic interdependence of the long-range interests of various groups. If we are to endure and grow as a nation, the things which unite us must become more important than those which divide" (CEA, 1949a, p. 9. This mutuality of interests and importance was a key to Keyserling's economic and social philosophy.

In his Special Message to the Congress, September 6, 1945, President Truman proposed economic policy after the surrender of Japan in August, 1945. The President indicated that veterans and farmers would be protected: that the economy must grow to avoid depression; but, also, that prices and wages should not be allowed to rise as wartime rationing and price ceilings were lifted so as to prevent inflation and to maintain purchasing power (Special Message, Sept. 6, 1945, p. 265). The Fair Labor Standards Act of 1938, which set up minimum wages, was one step to maintain purchasing power by increasing wages to over 40 cents an hour. Also, the President wished to avoid the 1920–1 inflation and asked that the stabilization boards allow restrictions to be lifted only as supply increases came about after the wartime reconversion was more firmly established. Despite these problems, the President called for a full employment economy (ibid, p. 279) in the postwar period, partly due to the belief of many that postwar periods brought about recession due to decreased military expenditures.

Keyserling, in an article in the *New York Times* (June 8, 1947, p. 2) indicated that depression was not necessary. The key was to maintain high consumption for high production and to voluntarily moderate wage and price increases plus temporary rent controls and an extension of social security, minimum wage legislation, and increased housing to decrease the housing shortage (ibid, p. 2). A basic question related to the proper balance between profits, prices, and wages to keep supply and demand in balance and to preserve prosperity and individual liberty (ibid, p. 4). The role of business, labor, and government were intertwined in those objectives by necessity, not by mere choice.

In a memo of August 14, 1948, Keyserling attacked the wage–price problem specifically. In a reply to a study by Donald Wallace, Keyserling stated that he agreed that price–wage–profit policies needed to be part of monetary and fiscal policies (Keyserling, memo, p. 2) as well as policies concerning the relative levels of consumption and investment (ibid, p. 5). However, Keyserling disagreed with Wallace's statement that in periods of maximum employment without inflation, the system was in balance and no price–wage–profit policies were necessary (ibid). There may be, to Keyserling, need for policies even if the economy is temporarily balanced. Keyserling argues,

> If we were to assume that the economy is "in balance" when prices are neither rising nor falling at maximum employment, we would be assuming that such a situation would be self-perpetuating ... or ... we would be assuming that no serious flaws would at that stage be discernable. I cannot agree with this on either theoretical or practical grounds because such things as ... collective bargaining and taxation and debt management and many other policies have to go forward under such periods. (ibid, p. 6)

Thus, even in good times, policies cannot be in abeyance because conditions do change and no situation is ever perfect.

By March, 1948, the price–wage situation was worsening as labor made wage demands and business reacted against them. The wage–price–profit analysis of Keyserling was still relevant. In a March, 1948 issue of *Harper's*, Keyserling attacked the problem again. He pointed out three fallacies: that past wage–price relationships are meaningful as models; or that some past period gave us a correct relationship; that prices, wages, profits are unrelated; or that prices, wages, profits are related and must *always* move in the same direction – that is, if profits fall for some reason, should wages be forced to fall (Keyserling, *Harper's*, 1948, p. 224). Economic conditions change and, thus, wage, price, profit relationships change. Nevertheless, to Keyserling, since all economic endeavors are for the purpose of production, distribution, and consumption, then profits, wages, prices are only the means for accomplishing these functions. The relationship of prices to wages to profits at any moment of time is an accident of the moment and subject to change over time as economic history and statistics indicate (ibid, p. 225). In the long run, however, there must be a reasonable relationship between the three, et alii.

Profits provide capital and incentive for increased capacity. Wages provide the purchasing power to consume the increased output. Prices determine the real amount of output that can be consumed of the increased output (ibid). Furthermore, if we need more steel, profits should be high enough to entice such additions to steel capacity. If we do not need more steel, profits can be lower. Thus, what do we want to accomplish is a vital question – more steel or the same amount of steel. Do we need more airfields or more electricity? Profit policies will help entice what we need or want, airfields or electricity. It was never novel to Keyserling that the traveler and the economy must know where they want to go before they discuss how to arrive there (Ibid, p. 226).

The problem of balance is more than an industry-by-industry problem. An increase in steel output means an increase in inputs into the steel industry – capital, labor, coal, transportation, demand, et cetera. Before steel expands, it must be confident that its supplies of inputs are available and that consumption demands are present. Thus, there must be a balance between investment, production, consumption, which relates to the profit wage, and price balance. The goals of private enterprise and the goals of public policy are not separate. Keyserling stresses the need for private enterprise correlated to the needs of public policy and to private reaction to those policies – a form of indicative planning and private enterprise. To Keyserling, such a view was necessary because, to him, political democracy and economic justice are not separable; and economic progress and economic stability are compatible, if not inseparable. Prices, wages, profits; purchasing power, consumption and production are integrated into economic fluctuations and into the need for economic stability. This, to Keyserling, was not new in economic analysis. It appears in the Classicalists such as Adam Smith and David Ricardo; the Socialists such as Karl Marx; the Austrians such as Bahm-Bawerk and von Hayek; and the modem economists such as J. M. Keynes.

The problem of the balance was not the direction of prices, wages, and profits, but the relationship between them. As pointed out in the *New York Times*, January 8, 1949, after 1929, the US had falling prices and a depressed economy. After 1932, the US had rising prices and an expanding economy. In the late 1920s, prices were stable, but something must have been wrong to bring about 1929 (Keyserling, *New York Times*, January 9, 1949, p. 2; Reprinted, *Congressional Record*, January 31, 1949). Thus, it is not trends in prices, wages, profits, but the relationships between them. If prices exceed wages and profits, consumption and output will fall. If profits rise faster than wages, output may be enticed faster than consumption, so overproduction followed by recession will occur. If wages rise and prices rise, the increased purchasing power of wages is diminished by inflated prices. Relationships, not individual trends, are vital (ibid). Of course, it might be argued that if consumption falls, so will prices. However, in reality, in recession prices often rise as prices are administered upward in certain, crucial industries to offset the decline in revenues for decreased consumption. This worsens the imbalance between prices, wages, and purchasing power. In order to solve *both* the problem of *balance* and the problem of *stability*, the National Prosperity Budget was described. The Budget would (1) estimate a few years ahead to benefit business plans for expansion; (2) provide for those funds through public policies – tax benefits, for example; and (3) analyze the wage, price, profit relationships needed to sustain the expansion of industry in particular and the economy in general. To accomplish these tasks, the Budget must have an objective analysis of the needed relationship between wages, profits, and incomes that would provide incentives for both the needed expansion and the purchasing power to consume the goods therefrom (ibid, p. 5). This is the interrelated goal of the National Prosperity Budget.

Both the goal of full employment and the goal of stability was not to be solved at one time and then held constant for the rest of time. In the long-run, "stability means constant growth," not cyclical variations in economic growth (US Congress, *Congressional Record*, June 17, 1948, pp. 1f). The evidence was clear to Keyserling that first, the best periods of economic growth (1939, 1946) showed that "advances in prices and in dollar incomes have been accompanied by large gains in employment, production, and standards of living" (ibid, p. 1). This means that as incomes are increasing, the economy continues to progress because the goods supplied can be bought and, thus, output continues. Second, economic balance is necessary because for sustained growth, profits, output, demand, incomes and employment must continue and grow. Profits provide for investment funds; investment funds provide for increases in output: wages determine consumer demand; and prices determine real purchasing power. Once again, the key is not the price movements, *per se*, but the relationships between the price movements and various sectors of the economy (ibid, p. 2). Third, there is no reason to believe that past growth trends limit present growth trends. Setting priorities and setting policies aimed at those priorities can increase the growth trends. A concentration upon needed areas of growth and upon more stimulative areas of growth can both increase growth rates and sustain them (Keyserling, *New York Times*, January 20, 1952, p. B5).

In an article in *Challenge* magazine (May/June, 1987), Keyserling related the needed balance in the economy to recent American economic history. From 1969 to 1985, poverty had increased from 24.1 million persons (12 percent) to 33.1 million persons (14.0 percent) (Challenge, 1987, p. 30). This was a secular increase in unemployment and poverty. Based on Keyserling's projections, the average unemployment rate of 6.2 percent for 1967 to 1986 was actually 8.9 percent, if part-time and discouraged workers are included (ibid, p. 33). If progress was to continue, these disbalances would result in overproduction and the resultant poverty of recession.

In the *Challenge* article, Keyserling indicated that it has been argued that the poor performance has been caused by inadequate investment or, to some, inadequate savings. This to Keyserling is an analytical error. The real problem is not inadequate investment, but inadequate demand. Let us look at some figures.

In the boom period from the last quarter of 1982 to the second quarter of 1984, the average real rate of growth of investment was 9.1 percent. In contrast, the rate of growth of consumption was 4.6 percent. In addition, the rate of growth of profits was 40.4 percent, but the rate of growth of wages was 5.3 percent. From the second to the fourth quarters of 1984, the economy slowed down and profits declined, Despite the decline in profits, real investment continued to increase at 9.7 percent whereas wages rose only by 3.8 percent. Subsequently, real investment dipped significantly to

2.2 percent from 1984 into 1986 (ibid, p. 31). The cause was a rate of growth of consumption (final demand) below that of increased production and productivity (investment). Two things can be learned from the above statistics. First, private investment is not dependent upon the growth of retained earnings or profits as investment, at first, continued after the profit decline. Second, private investment is inhibited not by lack of loanable funds, but by inadequate demand. When the investment rate began to dip, "Relatively more emphasis upon stimulating final demand, including evaluating the incomes of the poor and deprived, would have been much more helpful to private investment and to the whole economy" (ibid, p. 31). The increase in final demand would have kept investment increasing as increased demand could have taken off the market the increased supply of goods. In a stable growth economy, increases in demand are needed for increases in output. This is central to the growth theories of Alvin Hansen, Evsey Domar, Sir Roy Harrod, William J. Fellner, and others. It seems to have been completely lost on current policy makers, but it is nothing new in economic science.[4]

In relation to continued growth, Keyserling, since 1953, had always been critical of cutting back the economy to fight inflation. To Keyserling, such cuts do not decrease inflation, they add to it. When companies cut output, they operate less efficiently on the cost schedules. Also, when companies cut output, they lose revenues. Thus, in an attempt to maintain profit levels or to reestablish total revenue, they raise prices. The rise in prices adds to both inflation and unemployment. The correct policy would be to give incentives to increase output (as discussed in chapter 4) as increasing output puts a downward pressure on prices. The fiscal budget should be aimed at a continuation of increased output and increased demand, a central element of economic growth theory.

There is the argument that too rapid a wage increase is inflationary. This, however, is not a refutation of Keyserling's analysis. It is, instead, a vindication of it. Just as an inadequate growth in consumer demand can diminish sales, profits and investment, so can a too rapid increase in final demand drive up prices, drive down real profits or after wage-profits, and thus, diminish investment. The policy for this problem is not to decrease output, but to restrain price increases via restrained wage increases. To do otherwise is bad social justice and bad economic policy. For example,

> The official position from the 1960s forward ... was that excessive increases in wage rates were mainly responsible for price inflation. In consequence, the official formulas led to wage increases that did not even keep up with inflation, while price-makers benefited substantially from feeble restraints. Thus, enlarged economic imbalances combined with palpable injustice. We do need a voluntary incomes policy promulgated by the government, but only if it is responsive to the interincome relationships essential to progress and justice – that is consistent with and integrated with other aspects of a national economic and related social policy. (ibid, p. 35)

Growth, then, requires balances within the economy, the balance between increasing production and increasing consumption. As production continues to increase, and as consumption tends to increase in a proper relationship to production, more and more of the population may be and continue to be employed. Thus, progress continues and absolute poverty diminishes as the newly employed can consume the fruits of a growing society. The relation between profits, wages, prices, output and consumption is crucial. Economic theory has long taught that consumption was the ultimate raison d'être of production. Then, it must be realized that consumption must continue to grow as production continues to grow, given the constraints of full employment and given a wage–price policy that reflects productivity, not the sheer power of one group over another. Economic progress and economic justice are not at odds with one another. Given a correct economic balance, they are concurrent goals.

7
The Theoretical Analysis of Leon H. Keyserling and Economic Policy

Leon Keyserling was a Keynesian. He was also influenced by such persons as Rexford Tugwell of Columbia University who questioned the whole US ethos. Thus, with his Keynesian economic analysis, he had a moral commitment derived partly from Tugwell, but learned earlier from his own father. In the Conference of Economic Progress Report (1983) Keyserling indicated that the real message of Keynes was that "the maldistribution of income generated more savings than could be absorbed by investment, and that Government should draw down this excessive saving by public borrowing for purposes of public investment" (Keyserling, 1983, p. 8). Such a statement, to Keyserling, was relevant in 1930 and at the time of his death in 1987. In many ways, however, Keyserling was a rather iconoclastic Keynesian. Perhaps he saw Keynes' *The General Theory of Employment, Interest, and Money* (1936) clearer than most. The "gist" of Keynes to Keyserling was aggregate demand. The policy implication was to Keyserling that aggregate supply or growth should be full employment growth and that the private consumer and the public sector were the chief instruments in maintaining aggregate demand and purchasing power equal to the full employment growth of aggregate supply, employment, and prosperity. It is possible that Keyserling recognized or stressed that different sectors of the economy must grow in relation to one another more than did Keynes on both the micro and the macro level. However, Keynes did stress that aggregate demand must grow in relation to output. Certainly, Keyserling did stress that after reaching full employment, full employment growth over time must become the stress. This became a major emphasis of Keyserling along with his emphasis upon the relevant growth of the sectors of the economy in relation to one another. Below, I shall try to generalize on what I intuitively believe to be the basic analytical economic framework of Keyserling and, also, develop a policy model. Any errors of simplicity are mine, not Keyserling's.

In economic aggregate income theory, national income (Y) is equal to consumption, (C), private investment (I) and net public outlays (G) plus net exports minus imports (FE). Since we cannot control international flows (exports/imports) too easily, (as the 1970s, 1980s indicate), we will concentrate on the domestic income flows, C, I, G.

In the income formula, consumption is the largest single component (1988 = $3,326.4 billion) and government outlays are the second largest (1988 = $997.5 billion) and private investment is the smallest (1988 = $772.0 billion) (*Federal Reserve Bulletin*, July 1989, A 53). This is of significance because it points out that what keeps aggregate demand going is C + G. Also, as investment depends upon profits, it is consumption that gives investors profits by purchasing their goods. Thus, profits depend upon consumption, private and public. Thus, we have

(1) $Y = C + I + G$, and
(2) $I = f [.b(y), G]$

The "(y)" term after (.b) indicates that consumption is some part of, or function of, consumers' income, disposable income. In economics we call that function (f) the marginal propensity to consume (.b) and give it a statistically determined numerical value, but let us save ourselves from the mathematics of all that.

If the continuation of consumption is the real basis of the continuation of supply and the means of increasing that supply – investment – what is the means by which consumption is determined? Consumption is primarily determined by the aggregate demand of wage earners and salary earners. This last point gives us three essential keys to Keyserling's economic analysis and economic policy. First, the factors that allow for the continuation of consumption to absorb production are wages and salaries. Second, to increase consumption, it is necessary to make certain that income is distributed in such a way as to maximize that private consumption. For this reason and for reasons of social justice, Keyserling always developed policies to help the poor – for reasons of equity and for reasons of increasing their consumption so as to maintain production. Third, as economic theory has taught us for centuries, the reason for production is consumption. "Economic man" produces to consume. To consume, the consumer must have wages and salaries (w). Thus,

(3) $C = f(w)$

where the total amount of private consumption is some function (that marginal propensity to consume again) of wages, after taxes (disposable income). Here we see the build up in the Keyserling analytical interpretation of Keynes specifically and economics generally. To do this, I will simply reverse the order of the three simple formulas presented above:

(1) $C = f(w)$
(2) $I = f[.b(Y), G]$, and
(3) $Y = C + I + G$

Basically, to Keyserling, if private consumption (C) were not capable of consuming the full employment output of production in times of full employment growth, the government sector (G) would step in to complete the consumption of that output – the policy implication. If the professional economist finds the above simplification *too* simple, I am not at this writing talking exclusively to the professional economist. Many economists have forgotten the basics while concentrating upon the complexities. If I have sinned in the other direction, the lay reader may thank me.

The above simple analysis brings up the question of economic policy. How do we bring about full employment production (supply) and maintain consumption (C) and, as needed, government (G) to maintain high production through high consumption? To simplify that, I have developed a schematic model of economic policy. In it, economic policy involves long-range planning by government and by business for the maintenance of high production through high consumption and high prosperity. The Employment Act of

1946 and the Full Employment and Balanced Growth Act of 1978 plus Keyserling's concept of the National Prosperity Budget which is similar to the full employment budget concept utilized later by Walter Heller during the Kennedy administration are implied by the analysis.

The first step for planning (A, Figure 7.1) is to have the Council of Economic Advisors to develop a plan, A National Prosperity Budget for full employment and for full employment growth similar to that done during the Truman Administration and the Kennedy–Johnson Administration. These administrations, until the Viet Nam War brought inflation after 1966, had good growth records with low inflation, *simultaneously*. To Keyserling, the plan should have inputs

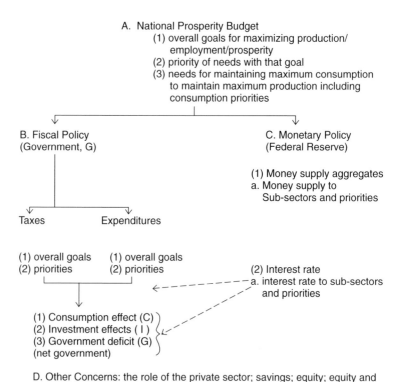

Figure 7.1   *Schematic model for economic policy*

from business, labor, agriculture, banking and finance, education, and other groups somewhat similar to the development of the "indicative plan" in France.

The plan should be both an aggregate plan for the entire economy and a disaggregated plan concerning how particular important sectors of the economy fit into the overall plan. For example, it may be that the overall plan called for a growth rate of, let us say, 5.5 percent to achieve and maintain full employment, growth of resources, and productivity. However, the steel industry, as an example, might have to grow at 6.5 percent or the steel industry may need complete revitalization. If so, that priority is spelled out and the measures needed – public and/or private – to accomplish that priority spelled out specifically enough for the purpose. Let us put off the various financial arrangements until our discussion of budgetary plans below. It might be that housing is in short supply. If so, a priority in the plan may be housing. How much housing? Housing for whom and where? Housing at what cost? How to be financed? Again let us discuss financing below. However, it should be stated that Keyserling was a strong and constant advocate of decent housing. Housing provides shelter for our citizens. It provides assets to our citizens. It provides jobs for the middle to lower skilled groups. It is, then, both needed to house the citizens and beneficial to employ the workers including the workers in home furnishings and home utilities and services. Keyserling often suggested that it would be a likely candidate to absorb much unemployment in recessions when other construction activities were declining. Thus, it could easily be a shelf of public works for a recession – planned in the expansion, put into operation in the recession.

The above indicates that the National Prosperity Budget was (1) for full employment growth. It was also (2) a general plan for the entire economy (or the major sectors of the economy – steel, housing, etc. – not the corner drugstore). Next, there would be (3) priorities within the plan – steel, housing, mass transit, conservation, etc – and (4) the means to get these priorities undertaken and financed, a problem discussed below. Basic to the continuation of growth, however, was (5) the premise that all sectors must grow in some proportion to each other. Profits were necessary, but must not impinge upon consumption. There must be some proportional growth between production – consumption; between wages, prices, profits. There was no magic "formula" for this, but the proportional relationship had to be recognized. Lastly, there must be the means (6) to monitor the plan for changing events. However, since the plan is primarily composed of goals without specific details about every detail (a major fault of Soviet over-planning, at least prior to Gorbachev's attempt at reforms) these modifications would not be difficult. The plan should be a plan, not a monument set in concrete. Note, too, that is a plan with goals and priorities. It is not a mere forecast based upon the mere extrapolation of the present into the future. A plan guides or gives priorities to the future.

The fiscal program (figure 7.1, B above) is of course designed by the Council of Economic Advisors and other bodies and presented to the President for his approval and modifications and then sent to Congress for its enactment and modifications. Naturally, the Chairman of the Council and other economic bodies in the executive branch would testify before Congressional committees on it as spokespersons for the President. The two major tools were taxes (T) and expenditures (E) with the net deficit, or surplus or balance being the result of the previous two (E – T) with the provision that the deficit should only be large enough to drive the economy towards full employment and full employment growth given the fiscal multipliers. Thus, the deficit, surplus, or balance is a residual of E and T but it should not be a random residual.

If actual output is below potential output, one way of stimulating the economy is to cut taxes. That method has been tried by Presidents Truman, Kennedy, and Reagan. All have been successful to a greater or lesser extent depending upon the circumstances. If the gap between actual output and potential output were $500,000,000, the needed decrease in taxes should be (circa) $166,000,000, assuming a tax multiplier of 3.

However, to Keyserling, a mere tax decrease is not enough. A tax decrease aims at the economy in general and may be successful, but the general expansion may overlook or not give enough emphasis to particular sections of the economy that need priority attention. Thus, Keyserling in his overall National Prosperity budget would use tax selectively aimed at specific parts of the economy. If the growing economy needed to revitalize the steel industry, then tax cuts or tax benefits for investors that affected the steel industry specifically could be used. Or if housing were in short supply, tax benefits for investors and/or consumers in that industry could be used. Such a program would both stimulate the general economy as well as the selected sectors of need or priority. These selected benefits would last until the need or priority was fulfilled. The selectivity would be part of the planning process that had been previously agreed upon by government, business, labor, agriculture, finance, and other relevant groups.

There is one other tax concept that we have not touched – the problem of social equity. To Keyserling, the tax cut should fall mostly on the lower and middle income groups because they are the poorest groups and need tax aid the most to maintain a decent living standard. That is the question of equity. However, by allowing them a decent living standard, one is also allowing them to consume more than before. Thus, purchasing power is also increased. If purchasing power (aggregate demand) is increased, so can aggregate output, employment and prosperity. Thus, the question of equity is tied to the problem of full employment via the concept of mass consumption. This is a phenomena that Keyserling believed was ignored or unrecognized by many policy makers.

Expenditures are also a part of the fiscal package of maintaining full employment growth. If, for example, the economy were $500,000,000 below full employment, the needed expenditure increase would be $142,857,000 (circa), assuming an expenditure multiplier of 3.5. Keyserling believed that expenditure increases had been utilized less than tax decreases in stimulating the economy. To him, the dependence upon tax reduction was an unfortunate economic policy bias for several reasons. First, the multiplier effect was greater for expenditures than for taxes. Second, an expenditure is an expenditure and can be spent where it is needed the most – steel, housing, energy, or whatever. A selected tax cut to stimulate those sectors may or may not do so or the time response may be slow. An expenditure can begin to stimulate it as soon as the expenditure has been made. If, for example, the nation needed more tanks, the Congress would probably spend the money to get them rather than cut taxes in that industry in hopes that someone might take the bait and produce more tanks.

When considering expenditures, the question of equity arises again. To increase the incomes of the poor, increases in expenditures to help the poor are necessary – social security, minimum wage, income supplements, unemployment compensation, etc. Thus, from an equity point of view, these expenditures are desirable. But these expenditures are also desirable from an economic point of view. Higher incomes to the under-privileged mean higher consumption by them which stimulates supply, employment (perhaps of the poor themselves to get themselves to get them off unemployment insurance), and increases the economy towards full production and full prosperity. Equity and mass consumption are not completely separated issues. For economic stability and growth, in a free enterprise system there must be a proportional growth of consumption with incomes and production. We will return to this problem, as Keyserling conceived of it, under "D" when we discuss the wage– price problem.

Monetary policy (Figure 7.1, C) would be handled differently than it has been since the "Accord" of 1951–2. There would be an increase in the money supply at a sufficient rate to maintain full employment growth. It would also be a money supply increase that would maintain low interest rates.

The preference for low interest rates is more, to Keyserling, than merely the market response to adequate increase in the money supply. The stress on low interest rates by Keyserling is due to the economic wisdom that low interest rates are an incentive to high investment. Low interest rates keep prices lower by keeping financing costs lower. Low interest rates do not transfer large amounts of wealth to the money-lending class. Low interest rates allow public and private expenses on other items that could not be made if these funds were used exclusively for interest payments. In 1989, for example, interest payments on the national debt were 14 percent of the outlays of the Federal Budget (*Federal Reserve Bulletin*, 1989, p. A29).

There is the conventional wisdom that an attempt to control inflation needs a decrease in the rate of growth of the money supply and a resultant increase in interest rates. Keyserling would disagree with this because inflation is usually accompanied by price increases in certain sectors of the economy (1970s, oil). Also, as prices are administered on certain important sectors of the economy, a general decrease in the money supply and a general increase in interest rates hurt all sectors, not merely the price-administered sectors that are the probable cause of the problem. The interest rate increase hurts the borrower-investor. The increased prices, due to administered pricing, hurts the consumer. The producer, by increasing his prices to offset diminished demand, escapes from receiving the full burden of contractionary policy. Keyserling would use selective credit controls to control those inflating sectors of the economy, or, even, selective interest rate increases for sectors expanding too rapidly. Were some sector, such as housing, lagging, there is no reason to decrease housing starts via high interest rates just because prices or wages are increasing in the steel industry. Selective policies can aim at the guilty without hitting the innocent. The decisions to use selective controls – when and where – would be part of the overall National Prosperity Budget and its priorities. Also for Keyserling, a less independent Federal Reserve is necessary for better long-term growth and lower interest rates.

The above stresses three points in regard to monetary policy. First, it should be based on a long-term (but not necessarily constant) increase in the money supply at low interest rates. Second, both in inflation and in recession, more use of selective controls should be utilized. Third, as we have seen in chapter 5, high interest rates to slow down growth result in low growth, higher finance costs, and higher inflation. An inflation, to Keyserling, is fought in the long run by increasing supply, not by decreasing demand. In the short run, selective controls over offending sectors of the economy and selective incentives toward priority sectors is a sounder version of monetary policy. To Keyserling, shortages, administered pricing, and slow growth of output were the main causes of inflation, not excess demand. Restricting output only increased prices, as his statistical analysis in chapter 5 indicates.

Section D of Figure 7.1 considers other important concerns of Keyserling that fit his general analysis: the role of the private sector; savings; equity and its connection with consumption; and wage–price policies.

To Keyserling, the role of the private sector in a free enterprise system was paramount. Keyserling had no desires for the socialization of private property. His interest was in reform. A major tool of this would be to involve the private sectors of the economy in the planning and priority process. This would allow the private sector to plan ahead with knowledge of what the economic plan is.

That would add a degree of certainty to the market. This would benefit the private sector. This does not replace the private sectors. Instead, it enhances their ability to react to and maintain a steady pace of investment.

Second, there is a problem of savings. Recently, there has been a great deal of discussion among investment economists and bankers that the American public must save more. The amount of savings out of disposable income is low, especially in comparison to other industrial countries. There is some doubt as to whether they count social security as savings, but that is not a point that would concern Keyserling. Keyserling would say that there are plenty of savings in the economy. To define the amount of savings, to Keyserling, one would not only measure the savings of individuals, one would measure the amount of retained earnings and other accounting procedures of corporations. One would also count the profit of all types of financial institutions from high interest rates. These forms of savings are large by any standards. But, in Keyserling's view, what if they are not large enough? If not, Keyserling asked, is not the Federal Reserve the "fiscal agent" of the United States? Like any other advanced nation, the Federal government has a central bank. If the Federal Reserve's "independence" allows the central bank to unduly restrict the money supply and drive up interest rates, then its "independence" should be more limited. To Keyserling, the Federal Reserve–Treasury Accord of 1951–2 which still dominates our thinking concerning the Federal Reserve was a mistake.

To Keyserling, equity was important. A decent society and an affluent society must help those who do not benefit from that affluence or growth. For the unemployed, there should be a higher level of unemployment compensation. Here, however, Keyserling would add that a full employment policy would diminish unemployment greatly. For the employed, there should be a minimum wage to maintain a decent standard of living and a high level of consumption. Also, over time, the minimum wage should at least keep up with increases in productivity so that its real purchasing power is maintained. In 1988, for example, one textbook author, in a general newsletter, indicated that from 1980 to 1988, median family income had increased from $29,700 to $32,000 (Schiller, 1988, p. 1). However, in a reply to my question, that author pointed out that there had been no compensation made for inflation in his figures. From 1980 to 1988, the rate of inflation was 18 percent. In real purchasing power terms, then, median family income had *decreased* from $29,700 in 1980 to $27,118 in 1988. Thus, median family income had lagged behind productivity increases or price increases. This is a problem of equity.

The equity problem is also a consumption problem. If real incomes are declining, the consumer has less real income to purchase the output of industry. If the consumer has less real purchasing power, eventually output will exceed demand. A recession is a result. So there is a tie between equity, mass consumption, and mass production. That tie is the income of consumers from which consumption is derived. Thus, there must be balances in the economy. The balance between consumption and production. The balance between investment increases and consumption increases. The balance is the relationship between wages, prices, and profits.

Lastly, the wage–price problem is of significance. As I indicate elsewhere, eminent economists such as Paul Samuelson have referred to this as the largest unsolved problem of capitalism (Brazelton, 1977, p. 8). A socialist leader of the 1980s might reply, "And of socialism, too."

The solution to Keyserling was clearly akin to that of Sweden just as his National Prosperity Budget was akin to French "indicative planning." Simply stated, Swedish wage policy sets wage increases in relation to productivity increases. If, for example, productivity is 5 percent, wage increases can be up to 5 percent. As a 5 percent increase in productivity is a 5 percent increase in output, a 5 percent increase in wages (the source of demand) is justifiable, and, also, necessary to absorb the additional output. As discussed in chapter 5, there are some technical problems here. If industry A had a 7 percent increase in productivity and industry B had a 3 percent increase in productivity, should a 5 percent rule be applied to both? If we allowed 5 percent to A and 3 percent to B, then there would be a redistribution of income from B workers to A workers. Is that fair? However, if both received 5 percent, profits in A would increase, but profits (after wages) in B would decrease. That might bankrupt B. But, then, why should a society subsidize an unproductive industry via low wages? In an economy such as Sweden (but also in economies such as the United States where export earnings are becoming more important), can the economy afford to tolerate an unprogress-ive industry such as B? Generally, the Swedes say "No." For reasons of simplicity, in his writings, Keyserling tended to agree.

Once again, we see the problem of balance manufacturing itself – the balance between aggregate output on the supply side and real income and the maintenance of purchasing power by means of an incomes policy on the demand side. For stability, the balance must be maintained – i.e., supply = demand, or more correctly, to Keyserling, as wages are the source of demand, demand = supply. Beyond mere stability and into the realm of continued full employment output, consumption and prosperity, the changes in aggregate demand must keep pace with the changes in aggregate supply. To be stable, an economy must have balance. To maintain growth, an economy must maintain balance. This is an essential message of Keyserling.

As indicated briefly in Chapter 4, at the occasion of the Thirtieth Anniversary of the Employment Act of 1946, the Joint Economic Committee of Congress held special hearings on the Employment Act (HJEC, 1976). Leon Keyserling, among others, was asked to testify. In his testimony (HJEC, 1976, pp. 298–307), Keyserling maintained that despite the good times for the American economy, the objectives of the Employment Act (and, thus, the potentials for the American economy) had not been obtained. In his verbal testimony, he cited eleven specific problems.

First, instead of positive programs and goals for the family, for business, and government, the "naysayers" have stressed how bad reality is and forecast the worst instead of designing meaningful and helpful policies and goals. Part of this is due to the estimates of potential economic growth being an average of 3 percent. However, Keyserling reminds us that the 3 percent is an average of periods of prosperity, recession and stagflation. To him, the potential growth of the economy is the prosperity period growth rate, not the one averaged down by recessionary growth rates – thus, instead of a 3 percent average, the potential, prosperity rate of growth is much higher and, thus, using it as a goal would result in both more output and less unemployment.

Second, without long-range goals, US economic policies and programs have been tardy, fragmentary, and, often, contradictory.

Third, both monetary and fiscal policy have been "indiscrim-inately applied aggregate and blunderbuss..." (ibid, p. 300). Instead of such indiscriminate policies, monetary and fiscal policies must have coordinated, long-term goals; and they must provide selective controls to stimulate what needs to be stimulated for the economic good, and de-stimulate what needs destimulating. In other words, "We must instead apply those policies in a more discerning and even selective manner to remedy distortions in the economy, and, thus, to achieve the balance of equilibrium relationships among the components required for sustained, full employment" (ibid). In other words, once again, we must not put air in the gas tank and oil in the radiator (ibid).

Fourth, we hear from the "naysayers" that both monetary and fiscal policies have failed. But they have failed because of their misuse. Aggregate monetary and fiscal policies should be accompanied by micro-economic training and employment programs to break bottlenecks and to diminish shortages – once again, discerning selectivity as well (ibid, p. 301).

Fifth, we need to destroy the myth that policies must remain neutral in terms of income redistribution. This has led economists to neglect both economic and social justice and has led to higher unemployment and lower production. Through intelligent and well-explained policy goals, the problem of income distribution can be alleviated. Still, however, Keyserling stressed growth for all rather than income redistribution in a stagnant economy, as his analysis of the correct goals for fiscal and monetary policy, as discussed above, indicate.

This last point is stressed in his sixth complaint. Therein, he states that: "The notion that we can fill the promise of America, extend sensible help to those in poverty and starvation everywhere with no growth or low growth is sensation-seeking nonsense" (ibid). Instead, we must aim for the growth of both output and employment in relation to the growth in our economic potential – resources, labor, capital and technology – over time.

Seventh, we must abandon "the veritable orgy of incontinent and inequitable tax reductions" (ibid). Keyserling favored tax reforms, but he also stressed that "to treat tax reduction and increased public investment as interchangeable or of equal value has been for many years, [sic] the most costly error of national economic policy (ibid). To build an adequate infra-structure for the economy is more important than a tax cut benefiting the many very little.

The previous point led to his point number eight. Therein, he indicated that we must stop our critique of public spending for mass transit, health services, environmental production, etc., and acting as if such public expenditures were of equal importance to tax cuts that increased the demand for private autos, cigarettes, and so on. Also, of course, expenditures for mass transit, health services, etc. add to output, welfare, and employment. In terms of cost-plus analysis, public health expenditures now are cheaper than an ill society later.

Ninth, the "free-wheeling" Federal Reserve must be answerable to the public. This, of course, goes back to Keyserling's critique of the "Accord." In his critique, he stressed the need for low interest rates and an adequate money supply for the purpose of continued economic growth. In a way, I believe he is correct. Modern economic analysis does stress that in order for output to grow, so must the money supply. In terms of economic growth analysis, the increase in the money supply allows for the new output to be both financed and consumed. Keyserling's view was more politicized than this analysis, but, nevertheless, a tight money supply with variable interest rates is dangerous in relation to continued, non-inflationary and non-recessionary, economic growth; but such long-term increases in the money supply should be within the limits of increases in economic potential, not mere political pressures.

Tenth, Keyserling attacked the "pernicious doctrine of the trade off" between inflation and unemployment – a doctrine that exists to the present but, in terms of low inflation and low unemployment at present (1998–2000), seems to be weakened.

Similarly, Keyserling pointed out in his 1976 testimony, that in 1965, the Council of Economic Advisers under Walter Heller had reduced unemployment from 6.8 percent to 3.5 percent, and had maintained inflation at only 1.5 percent. Clearly to Keyserling, low unemployment did not bring inflation, a priori. Indeed, to Keyserling, economic growth and low employment periods in American economic history had brought price stability – "empirical observation of the economy in action since 1953 demonstrates conclusively that a strong and healthy economy is accompanied by more price stability than a weak and sick economy" (ibid, p. 302). Thus, the trade-off theory is false as recent data seems to help confirm.

Eleventh, we should not leave it to the President, the Council of Economic Advisers, the Federal Reserve to determine what the growth rate and unemployment rate was to be and, thus, what is good for us. Instead, the Congress should "define national values, including the allowable limits of unemployment, and then tell the experts that it is their job to help devise methods to get unemployment down to that level" (Ibid). This would, to Keyserling, employ macro-economic policies and selective micro-economic policies, and, in terms of the vocabulary of 1998–2000, substitute secrecy for the transparency that is vital to a participatory democracy. Such a Congressional "mandate" would substitute the secret plans of the Administration of the day for a known, stated policy of an economy growing at its full economic potential over time. This, to him, strengthens both democracy and capitalism within the constraints of rationality.

To me, there is a problem with such Congressional "mandates" suggested by Keyserling in 1976. In the 1980s, the Congress and the President presided over the largest increases in Federal deficits in recent history; and in the 1990s, Congress passed tax legislation favorable to the upper income classes. One Congressman suggested that the Federal Reserve should be interested primarily and solely in controlling inflation, not economic growth or employment. My own "lesson learned" from the recent history is that perhaps, despite Keyserling's view on the subject, that the Federal Reserve is more reliable than Congress in setting goals as the Federal Reserve (although not perfect) is not a political organization, a priori, and Congress is. The Federal Reserve actions and goals should not be tightly held secrets, but transparency can apply to the Federal Reserve just as it can apply to Congress in terms of an overall goal or goals. Thus, full employment, price-stable growth, a la Keyserling, can still be a recognized goal.

The concept of economic growth in terms of fulfilling our full employment growth potential, a la Keyserling, has so far been analyzed in terms of the domestic economy, its problems, and potential. The concept does have international trade and international power ramifications as well. A highly productive, fully employed domestic economy can increase its trade abroad; sell its output surpluses abroad as exports to gain foreign exchange for needed or desired imports; increase its international prestige; and increase or maintain its ability to tax for both domestic purposes and defense purposes.

That last point was touched upon in a brief paper at the Harry S. Truman (Presidential) Library by Donald K. Pickens (Pickens, 1975). Therein, it was pointed out that economic growth both strengthened our domestic economy and, thus, our ability to challenge our adversaries abroad. Pickens indicated that Keyserling believed that economic growth could increase our ability to finance and pay off any budget deficits needed to finance growth. In terms of the struggle between the Soviet Union and "Communism" versus the United States, Western Europe and "Capitalism", the growth concepts of Keyserling and others paid off in the long run. High growth rates helped to finance the military expenditures to counteract Soviet threats, real or perceived. Eventually, especially after 1968, US defense expenditures were attempted to some extent to be matched by Soviet defense expenditures at a higher relative cost to the Soviets as their growth rates declined. The final result was the collapse of the Soviet Union and "Communism" in 1991 and the retreat from Eastern Europe beginning in 1989 (for this and other reasons). US growth potential has surpassed their growth potential, especially after 1968 when their economic and social system became overplanned, stagnant, and moribund compared to the US's. Growth with relatively stable prices and full employment potential and reasonable fiscal/monetary policies aided in US perseverance. Since 1982, the American economy has continued to grow. The Russian economy is still below what it was in the late 1980s. Thus, growth has its pay-offs, now and in the future. Keyserling's growth emphasis was correct. Capitalism prospered and won.

The economic policies – macro and micro – of Keyserling were aimed at an economic growth rate of high output growth, high employment and low inflation. High output growth and high employment increases supply while high employment at reasonable and decent wages increases demand to absorb that increased supply at efficient levels along the cost curves to help keep inflation low. Thus, to Keyserling, growth was and is the key to the continued economic prosperity and power of the American economy and the American people and for the rest of the world. Keyserling stressed economic growth, but he did not forget the socio-economic balance needed between economic growth and equity. These were the vital parts in the purpose of Keyserling and of his economic analysis; and we could in the present learn much from him.

Appendix 1
The Concept of Economic Growth in Economic Analysis

Leon Keyserling is not alone in his advocation of a more responsive economic policy based upon the full employment budget concept where economic growth balances the budget at full employment. Keyserling, in his writings, called for a return to the active full employment budget concept of the Council of Economic Advisers under himself and later, under Walter Heller. James Tobin, the 1981 Nobel Prize recipient in Economic Science, called for the same thing.

To Tobin, as to Keyserling, the restrictive policies to prevent inflation have restricted potential output and raised unemployment (Tobin, 1986, p. 5). From this scenario, has come, Tobin suggests, the inflation-safe natural rate of unemployment. However, to Tobin, the inflation-safe natural rate of unemployment, cannot be reduced without structural changes in the economy as well as a better management of monetary and fiscal policy in relation to demand management in relation to the Employment Act of 1946. The correct policy should not be the policy of the Reagan years (1981–9) where the Federal Reserve tightened monetary policy and raised interest rates to diminish the inflationary effects of the building of the Federal deficit from 900 billion dollars in 1980 to 2.8 trillion dollars in 1988. To Tobin, such a

> tight-money/easy-budget combination is not viable in the long-run. It results in real interest rates on public debt higher than the sustainable growth rate of the economy. This is a recipe for an unending rise in the debt-to-GNP ratio, especially because the primary budget is also in deficit. The policy mix runs counter to long-run growth because it encourages present-oriented uses of GNP relative to future-oriented ones. The mix has resulted in a large current-account deficit in U.S. international transactions, i.e., in massive net borrowing from the rest of the world. (Ibid, p. 12)

With emphasis upon long-term growth and a more rational approach to the budget and the need for monetary policy and lower interest rates, Keyserling would agree. It is his analysis of balance and his analysis of economic progress with social justice – the growth continuum of production, consumption, jobs! As I also point out in the *Atlantic Economic Journal*, this emphasis upon growth involved an early use of the concept of a full employment budget (Brazelton, 1978, p. 32).

Tobin has to answer an essential question in his desire to get away from the high employment levels caused by the "inflation-safe unemployment rate" of recent theoretical analysis. Tobin's suggestions were aimed at the structure of the economy:

> improvements in public education; relaxation of minimum wage laws and other regulations that limit the downward flexibility of wages *and prices* [my emphasis]; encouragement of labor contracts that relate wages to firms' revenues, profits, or labor productivity; penalizing by unemployment-insurance surtaxes those employers who raise wages while they are curtailing employment or while unemployment is high in their localities; and annual economy-wide guideposts for wages and prices, with compliance induced by tax-based rewards and penalties. (Tobin, 1986, p. 6)

While Keyserling might argue with Tobin as to the specifics, Tobin is going in a direction similar to Keyserling. But where would Keyserling go himself in reestablishing the Employment Act of 1946?

To Keyserling, the Employment Act of 1946 has had its successes and failures (*Atlantic Economic Journal*, March 1978). However, the Council of Economic Advisers must change its current policy emphasis towards realism and growth (*Atlantic Economic Journal*, March 1980). First, to Keyserling the statistical analysis of the Council should be used to describe the actual economy of today, not to validate Neo-Classical economic theories. Second, the Council should reject the "trade-off" between inflation–employment as the failure it is – to decrease inflation, output and employment is restricted, but, as Keyserling had stated before, such policies add to inflation, not diminish it and restrict long-term growth, the real cure of inflation. The Council should recognize "economic balance" and the role of "income distribution" in maintaining vital policies – profits, wages, prices, production, consumption. Also, the Council must recognize that its fiscal policies have failed not because they are outmoded, but because they have put too much differentiation between the micro economy and the macro economy.

> the use of fiscal and monetary policies have fallen short because they have been misapplied. Among other evils, this has led to an excessive insistence that so-called micro-economic or structural policies should be substituted as our main additional reliance now. But the distinction between conventional policies and structural policies is substantially overplayed; the two overlap, once it is recognized that fiscal and monetary policies should pay more attention to composition and balance. And even when the effort is to generate more employment and less unemployment by structural policies, nobody can be employed (without taking the job away from someone else) without the needed increase in

total outlays ... All empirical evidence indicates that structural employment is reduced when the nation is pursuing a general full employment
policy. (Keyserling, *Atlantic Economic Journal*, March, 1980, p. 21).

Appendix 2
Brief Chronology and Biographical References by Leon H. Keyserling (Edited: W. Robert Brazelton)

Born, January 22, 1908, Charleston, South Carolina

Resided on St. Helena Island and later in Beaufort, South Carolina, until his graduation from high school

Graduation, Columbia College, New York, 1928

Graduation, Harvard Law School, 1931

Taught at Columbia College and worked for Rockefeller Foundation on "Education," 1931–3. Co-authored, 1932, *Redirecting Education*, Columbia University Press, 1934

Rexford Tugwell calls Keyserling to Washington, 1933

1933–7, Legislative Assistant, Senator Robert Wagner (D., NY), and adviser to Senator Wagner until Wagner's death in 1946. Principal draftsman under Senator Wagner and in the Roosevelt administration: $3,300,000,000 public works bill; the wage and hour collective bargaining sections of the National Industrial Recovery Act, 1935; the National Labor Relations Act (Wagner Act), 1935; the US Housing Act of 1937 (slum clearance and low rent housing); the Employment Act of 1946; the General Housing Act of 1949; a consultant to Senator Robert Wagner, Senator Allen J. Ellender, and Senator Robert Taft; and a principal draftsman for the Full Employment and Balanced Growth Act, 1978 (the Humphrey-Hawkins Act)

1935–7, expert, US Senate Committee on Banking and Currency

1936, 1940, 1944, writer for the Democratic Platform Committee, under chairman of the Platform Committee, Senator Robert Wagner; drafted Executive order creating Wartime National Planning Agency (forerunner of the Department of Urban Development, HUD)

1942–6, Acting Administrator of Housing Agencies (nine years in all; including previous work); General Consul, National Housing Agency

1944, Second Prize ($10,000) Pabst Essay Contest on Post-War Full Employment; became the basis for the Employment Act of 1946

1946–9, Vice Chairman, Council of Economic Advisers to the President; 1947, Acting Chairman, 1950–3, Chairman

1953–71, private consultant: represented 13 utilities before federal and state regulatory agencies; public employee agencies, New York City; served as an adviser to the government of India; Puerto Rico; and Israel (1961–5, president, National Committee for Labor Israel)

1971 and thereafter, voluntary consulting, public service and testimony before Congressional committees

Appendix 3
Other Related Articles, Not Quoted Herein (But Presented to Author by Leon Keyserling)

Newspapers and journals

Editors, Challenge Magazine, (1976) "The Full Employment and Balanced Growth Act of 1976," *Challenge Magazine*, September/October pp. 21–31.

Keyserling, Leon H., (1945) "From Patchwork to Purpose," *Survey Graphic*, March.

Keyserling, Leon H., (1950) "Planning for a $300 Billion Economy," *New York Times*, Section B, June 18, p. 9.

Keyserling, Leon H., (1953) "Editorial – The Role of the Council," *New York Journal of Commerce*, May 13.

Keyserling, Leon H., (1953) Letter to the Editor – "Keyserling Defends Position on Economic Council's Role," *New York Journal of Commerce*, May 12.

Keyserling, Leon H., (1957) "The Case for a Big Budget," *New York Times Magazine, New York Times*, February 3.

Keyserling, Leon H., (1958) "Next Step – A 600 Billion Dollar Economy?" *New York Times Magazine*, November 23.

Keyserling, Leon H., (1960) "Public Wealth – and Private, Too," *New York Times Magazine, New York Times*, August 21, Section F, Part 1.

Keyserling, Leon H., (1966) A Book Review, (*The Guaranteed Income: Next Step in Economic Evolution?* Robert Theobald, Editor), entitled "Something for Everybody," *New York Times Magazine, New York Times*, February 27, Section F, Part 1.

Keyserling, Leon H., (1968) "The Skirmish Line," *Journal of Commerce*, Tuesday, December 10.

Keyserling, Leon H., (1981) "International Implications of U. S. Economic Performance And National Priorities," *Atlantic Economic Journal* (Atlantic Economic Society), December, pp. 27–34.

Keyserling, Leon H., (1983) "U. S. Economy, Performance and Prospects, and Needed Corrective Policies," *Atlantic Economic Journal*, (Atlantic Economic Society), September, pp. 9–44.

Keyserling, Leon H., (1986) Letters – "Bishops' Letter Offers an Economic Solution," *New York Times*, Tuesday, December 16.

Keyserling, Leon, (1986) "Response: Let's Get This Straight (A Reply to Walter Heller, *Challenge Magazine*, March/April 1986), *Challenge Magazine*, November/December, pp. 56–8.

Keyserling, Leon, (1987) "Will it Be Progress or Poverty?" *Challenge Magazine*, May/June, pp. 30–6.

Richey, John C., (1977) "We Can Have Full Employment Without Inflation," *St. Petersburg Times*, Sunday, March 27, 3D.

Richey, John C., (1978) Letters, "Wage and Price Control *CAN* Work," *St. Petersburg Times*, April 17.

Santoni, G. J., (1980) "The Employment Act of 1946: Some History Notes," *Review*, Federal Reserve Bank of St. Louis, Vol. 68, No. 9, November, pp. 5–15.

Virgo, John M., (1987) "Leon H. Keyserling, 1908–1987," *Atlantic Economic Journal*, (Atlantic Economic Society), September, p. 1.

Weidenbaum, Murry L., (1976) "The Case Against the Humphrey-Hawkins Bill," *Challenge Magazine*, September/October, pp. 21–3.

Various publications

Blough, Roy, (1950) "Fiscal Policy in a Defense Economy," *National Tax Journal*, Vol. III, December 1950, pp. 273–82 (attached: "Taxes Be Increased? – Recognize The Cost of What We Buy," Roy Blough.)

Casebeer, Kenneth M., (1987) "Holder of the Pen: An Interview with Leon Keyserling on Drafting the Wagner Act," *University of Miami Law Review*, Vol. 42, November, pp. 285–363.

Committee on Labor and Public Welfare, (1976) Full Employment and Balanced Growth Act, 1976, Hearings, May 14, 17–19, pp. 72–140.

Joint Economic Committee, (1969) "The Employment Act: Twenty Years of Policy Experience," Chapter 7. pp. 170–86.

Keyserling, Leon H., (1949) "Development and Works Program, December 7, 1949; *Report of the Council of Economic Advisers to the President*, Fourth Annual Report, December, 1949, "Business and Government".

Keyserling, Leon H., (1950) "Letter to Seymour Harris," December 15.

Keyserling, Leon, (1960) "Selected Comments on LHK Studies – Food and Freedom – October 1960," December.

Keyserling, Leon H., (1964) "Early Comments on 'Two Top Priority Programs to Reduce Unemployment', (published December 1963)," January.

Keyserling, Leon H., (1967) "Review: The 'New Economics' Not New Enough," Tobin, *National Economic Policy*, Heilbroner, *The Limits of American Capitalism*, *Yale Law Journal*, Vol. 78, July.

Keyserling, Leon H., (1976) "Presentation of Leon H. Keyserling at Conference Marking Thirtieth Anniversary of Employment Act of 1946," P. M. Friday, March 19.

Keyserling, Leon H., (1978) "Ode, Long Before Achieving Immortality, If Ever, But My 70th Birthday, Nonetheless," read at dinner party, January 22.

Keyserling, Leon H., (1979) "Comments by Leon H. Keyserling," Conference, May.

Keyserling, Leon H., (1981) Letter to W. Robert Brazelton, February 25.

Keyserling, Leon H., (1984) "A Close Up Appraisal of Harry S. Truman with Accent Upon Economic Policy," Address at Truman Centennial, Kansas City, Missouri, March 1.

Keyserling, Leon H., (1986) "Record of Leon H. Keyserling in Re (letter to) Economics and Social Programs," Employment Act of 1946, February 4.

Keyserling, Leon H., (1987) "The Money Problem and the Economic Problem," Address of Leon H. Keyserling, Thirteenth Annual Convention, Eastern Economic Association, Thursday, March 5.

Lewis, J., and Schultze, C., (1952) "To the Council," September 29.

Lewis, John P., (1953) "A Proposal for Work in the Field of Wage-Profit Relations...," January 19.

Nourse, Edwin G., (1956) "Defining Our Employment Goals Under the 1946 Act," *Review of Economics and Statistics*, Vol. 38, May.

Public Papers of the Presidents, Harry S. Truman, (1945) September 6 (128), 1945, pp. 263–307; Special Message to the Congress Presenting a 21-Point Program for the Reconversion Period.

Major publications

Ten lead articles, the *New York Times*
Thirty monographs, as director, Conference on Economic Progress

Awards

Honorary Degrees
  Bryant College
  University of Missouri-Kansas City
Honorary Membership
  Faculty, Industrial College of the Armed Forces; Special Award, 1983
Centennial Celebration of Mayor: Fiorello H. LaGuardia; and National Press Club The Martin Luther King, Jr., Center for Social Change, 1979
American Jewish Council, New York, NY and Washington, DC: Man of the Year Pabst Brewers, The Pabst Essay Award, "The American Economic Goal: A Practical Start Toward Postwar Full Employment" (See Chapter III)

There were several voluntary testimonial statements from prominent Senators concerning Leon Keyserling's service to his country, as presented to me by Keyserling himself. For example: Senator Harry F. Byrd, Chairman of the Senate Finance Committee (D, Virginia) indicated his sometimes disagreement with Keyserling, but, nevertheless, invited his testimony before his important Committee, in recognition of his expertise. Senator Robert A. Taft (R, Ohio) indicated Keyserling's abilities and accuracies in his analysis and, while he and many of his Republican colleagues disagree with

Keyserling, he has always fairly considered their views. Senator Hubert Humphrey, Chairman, Joint Economic Committee (D, Minnesota) indicated that he had often learned more economics from Keyserling in five minutes than from all the other economists who testified in front of his Committee, an important Committee of the Senate. Later, Senator Humphrey (the Democrat Presidential Candidate in 1968, losing to Richard Nixon) indicated that Keyserling wanted a better life for all Americans. That better life for all Americans was the purpose of Keyserling's belief in economic growth, economic balance, and economic equality and justice. It was also the essence and purpose of the man.

Appendix 4
Book-Length Publications of Leon H. Keyserling With the Aid of Mary Dublin Keyserling (Conference on Economic Progress, Washington, DC)

Toward Full Employment and Full Production	July 1954
National Prosperity Program for 1955	February 1955
Full Prosperity for Agriculture	November 1955
The Gaps in Our Prosperity	September 1956
Consumption – Key to Full Prosperity	May 1957
Wages and the Public Interest	January 1958
The "Recession" – Cause and Cure	June 1958
Toward a New Farm Program	December 1958
Inflation – Cause and Cure	July 1959
The Federal Budget and "The General Welfare"	December 1959
Tight Money and Rising Interest Rates	July 1960
Food and Freedom	October 1960
Jobs and Growth	May 1961
Poverty and Deprivation in the U.S.	April 1962
Key Policies for Full Employment	September 1962
Taxes and the Public Interest	June 1963
Two Top-Priority Programs to Reduce Unemployment	December 1963
The Toll of Rising Interest Rates	August 1964
Progress or Poverty	December 1964
Agriculture and the Public Interest	February 1965
The Role of Wages in a Great Society	February 1966
A "Freedom Budget" for All Americans	Fall, 1996
Goals for Teachers' Salaries in our Public Schools	December 1967
Achieving Nationwide Educational Excellence	December 1968
Taxation of Whom and for What	December 1969
Growth with Less Inflation or More Inflation Without Growth	December 1970
Wages, Prices and Profits	December 1971
The Coming Crisis in Housing	December 1972

The Scarcity School of Economics	December 1973
Full Employment without Inflation	January 1975
Toward Full Employment within Three Years	January 1976
The Humphrey-Hawkins Bill "Full Employment and Balanced Growth Act of 1977"	February 1978
Goals for Full Employment and How to Achieve Them Under the "Full Employment and Balanced Growth Act of 1978"	February 1978
"Liberal" and "Conservative" National Economic Policies and Their Consequences, 1919–79	September 1979
Money, Credit, and Interest Rates: Their Gross Mismanagement by the Federal Reserve System	April 1980
How to Cut Unemployment to Four Percent and End Inflation and Deficits by 1987	February 1983

Notes

1. It can be pointed out that during much of this period, real wages were higher in America than in Europe (an economic incentive to immigration). It can also be noted that wages and growth are both important. If growth is profitably taking place, higher wages can be paid. There is no absolute "iron law." Productivity and technology and growth are also variables in the process.

2. As to Alvin Hansen's importance in economic circles for many decades, one has only to refer to his many editions of the very popular text, *A Guide to Keynes*. One can also refer to the Dissertation of W. Robert Brazelton, University of Oklahoma, Norman, Oklahoma; and the Dissertation on Mary Dublin Keyserling by Willadee Gillan Wehmeyer, University of Missouri-Kansas City.

3. In a pre-cursor to a similar point made by Lord Keynes, Tugwell wrote in terms of individual interests obstructing the evolution of true rationality whereas Keynes talked in terms of economics of today being over influenced by the economic scribblings of long dead economists (Tugwell, 1935, p. 404).

4. In class, I have begun to explicitly point out a national policy "fallacy of composition" as it is called in introductory economics classes. For example, on the micro-level, it makes economic sense to cut wages (if possible) to decrease costs, increase profits and, hopefully, investment. However, on the macro-level, to decrease wages decreases consumption which decreases sales, profits, investment, and national income and product to the detriment of the nation and the overall (macro) economy. Such a "fallacy of composition" may be America's "economic policy malaise."

Bibliography

Blough, Roy. (1950) "Fiscal Policy in a Defense Economy." *National Tax Journal*, Vol. III, December: pp. 273–82.

Board of Governors, (1990) *Federal Reserve Bulletin*, Washington, DC: January, A-29.

Brazelton, W. Robert. (1961) *A Critical Comparison of the Growth Theories of Alvin H. Hansen and William J. Fellner.* Dissertation. Norman: University of Oklahoma.

Brazelton, W. Robert. (1977) "Some Major Changes in the Principles of Economics as Exemplified by the *Principles of Economics* by Paul Samuelson 1948–73. *American Economist*, Fall: pp. 3–11.

Brazelton, W. Robert. (1978) "The Keyserling Years and Economics of Leon H. Keyserling." (Abstract). *Atlantic Economic Journal*, Vol. VI, March: p. 52.

Brazelton, W. Robert. (1980/81) "A Survey of Some Textbook Misinterpretations of Keynes." *Journal of Post Keynesian Economics*, Vol. III, Winter, pp. 256–70.

Brazelton, W. Robert. (1993) "Hansen: on Keynes, Hayek, and Commons." *Journal of Economic Issues*, pp. 940–8.

Brazelton, W. Robert. (1989) "Alvin Harvey Hansen: Economic Growth and a More Perfect Society." *The American Journal of Economics and Sociology*, Vol. 48, October: pp. 427–40.

Brazelton, W. Robert, and Wehmeyer, Willadee. (1989) *Leon H. Keyserling and Mary Dublin Keyserling, Growth and Equity: Over Fifty Years of Economic Policy And Analyses. From Roosevelt and Truman to Bush.* A study for and on deposit at the Truman Memorial Library, Independence, Missouri, USA.

Brazelton, W. Robert. (1994) "An Empirical Note on Deficits, Interest Rates and International Capital Flows: A Comment." *The Quarterly Review of Economics and Finance.*

Brown, Edmund (Governor, D, CA). (1964) "How to Put States Back in Business." *Harper's Magazine*, Vol. 229, No. 1372, September: pp. 98–103.

Casebeer, Kenneth M. (1987) "Holder of the Pen: An Interview With Leon Keyserling on Drafting the Wagner Act." *University of Miami Law Review*, Vol. 42, November: pp. 285–363.

Cebala, Richard and Koch, James. (1989) "An Empirical Note on Deficits, Interest Rates, and International Capital Flows." *Quarterly Review of Economics and Finance*, Vol. 29, Autumn: pp. 121–6.

Collins, Robert. (1989) "Leon Keyserling and Economic Growth." Unpublished paper Presented at the Organization of American Historians, April, 1989. On deposit at the Truman Memorial Presidential Library, Independence, Missouri, USA.

Colm, Gerhard. (1956) *The Employment Act, Past and Future*. National Planning Association, Washington, DC (now the National Policy Association).

Council of Economic Advisers (CEA). (1947a) *Economic Report of the President*, January 8, 1947. Washington, DC: US Government Printing Office.

Council of Economic Advisers (CEA). (1947b) *Midyear Economic Report of the President*, July 21, 1947. Washington, DC: US Government Printing Office.

Council of Economic Advisers (CEA). (1948a) *Economic Report of the President*, January, 1948. Washington, DC: US Government Printing Office.

Council of Economic Advisers (CEA). (1948b) *Midyear Economic Report of the President*, July, 1948. Washington, DC: US Government Printing Office.

Council of Economic Advisers (CEA). (1949a) *Economic Report of the President*, January, 1949. Washington, DC: US Government Printing Office.

Council of Economic Advisers (CEA). (1949b) *Midyear Economic Report of the President*, July 11, 1949. Washington, DC: US Government Printing Office.

Council of Economic Advisers (CEA). (1950a) *Economic Report of the President*, January 6, 1950. Washington, DC: US Government Printing Office.

Council of Economic Advisers (CEA). (1950b) *Midyear Economic Report of the President*, July 26, 1950. Washington, DC: US Government Printing Office.

Council of Economic Advisers (CEA). (1951a) *Economic Report of the President*, January 12, 1951. Washington, DC: US Government Printing Office.

Council of Economic Advisers (CEA). (1951b) *Midyear Economic Report of the President*, July 23, 1951. Washington, DC: US Government Printing Office.

Council of Economic Advisers (CEA). (1952a) *Economic Report of the President*, January 16, 1952. Washington, DC: US Government Printing Office.

Council of Economic Advisers (CEA). (1952b) *Midyear Economic Report of the President*, July, 1952. Washington, DC: US Government Printing Office, 1952.

Council of Economic Advisers (CEA). (1953) *Economic Report of the President*, January, 1953. Washington, DC: US Government Printing Office.

Council of Economic Advisers (CEA). (1954) *Economic Report of the President*, January, 1954. Washington, DC: US Government Printing Office.

Eckstein, Otto (an interview by Charles Alexander). (1982) "The Elusive Recovery." *Time*. Vol. 120, No. 6, December 27: pp. 60–2.

Editors. *Challenge Magazine*. (1976) "The Full Employment and Balanced Growth Act Of 1976." *Challenge Magazine*. September/October: pp. 21–31.

Federal Reserve Bank. (1989) *Federal Reserve Bulletin*. Washington: Board of Governors of the Federal Reserve, September, July.

Flash, Edward S. (1965) *Economic Advice and Presidential Leadership*. New York: Columbia University Press.

Galbraith, John Kenneth. (1981) *A Life in Our Times*. Boston: Houghton-Mifflin.

Gates, Robert Joseph. (1968) *The Role of the First Council of Economic Advisers* (Masters Thesis). Kansas City, Missouri: University of Missouri-Kansas City.

Hall, Robert E. (1993) "Macro Theory and the Recession of 1990–91." *American Economic Review*, Vol. 83, No. 2, May: pp. 270–4.

Hamby, Alonzo. (1973) *Beyond the New Deal: Harry S. Truman and American Labor.* New York: Columbia University Press.

Hansen, Alvin H. (1939) "Progress and Declining Population Growth." *American Economic Review*, Vol. 29, March: pp. 1–7.

Hansen, Alvin H. (1953) *A Guide to Keynes*. New York, New York: Mc-Graw-Hill.

Humphrey, Hubert. (1976) "The New Humphrey-Hawkins Bill." *Challenge*, May/June: pp. 21–9.

Keynes, John Maynard. (1936) *The General Theory of Employment, Interest and Money*. New York: Harcourt-Brace.

Keyserling, Leon H. (1944) "The American Economic Goal: A Practical Start Towards Post War Full Employment" (The Pabst Essay). Council of Economic Advisers Papers on Deposit, Truman Memorial Presidential Papers, Independence, Missouri, USA.

Keyserling, Leon H. (1947) "Must We Have Another Depression." *New York Times*, June 8: Reprinted *Congressional Record*, June 10, 1947.

Keyserling, Leon H. (1948a) "Memo to Donald Wallace of August 14, 1948: The Council and Committee on Wage-Price Relations." On Deposit, Truman Memorial Presidential Library, Independence, Missouri, U.S.A.

Keyserling, Leon H. (1948b). "For a National Prosperity Budget." *New York Times*, January 8: Reprinted, *Congressional Record*, January 31.

Keyserling, Leon H. (1948c) "Everybodies Probem: Press, Wages, Profits." *Harpers* Magazine, March: pp.221–28.

Keyserling, Leon H. (1949) "The Economic Test: Will We Act on Time?" *New York Times*, June 13: Reprinted *Congressional Record*, January 31.

Keyserling, Leon H. (1952) "New Challenges to the Economist." *New York Times*, January 20: Section B.

Keyserling, Leon H. (1956) *The Gaps in Our Prosperity*. Washington, DC: Conference on Economic Progress, (On Deposit, Truman Memorial Presidential Library, Independence, Missouri, USA).

Keyserling, Leon H. (1957) *Consumption – Key to Full Prosperity*. Washington, DC: Conference on Economic Progress, (On Deposit, Truman Memorial Presidential Library, Independence, Missouri, USA).

Keyserling, Leon H. (1958a) *Toward a New Farm Program*. Washington, DC: Conference on Economic Progress, (On Deposit, Truman Memorial Presidential Library, Independence, Missouri, USA).

Keyserling, Leon H. (1958b) *The Recession – Cause and Cure*. Washington, DC: Conference on Economic Progress, (On Deposit, Truman Memorial Presidential Library, Independence, Missouri, USA).

Keyserling, Leon H. (1959a) *Inflation – Cause and Cure*. Washington, DC: Conference on Economic Progress, (On Deposit, Truman Memorial Presidential Library, Independence, Missouri, USA).

Keyserling, Leon H. (1959b) *The Federal Budget and "The General Welfare"*. Washington, DC: Conference on Economic Progress, (On Deposit, Truman Memorial Presidential Library, Independence, Missouri, USA).

Keyserling, Leon H. (1960a) *Tight Money and Rising Interest Rates*. Washington, DC: Conference on Economic Progress, (On Deposit, Truman Memorial Presidential Library, Independence, Missouri, USA).

Keyserling, Leon H. (1960b) *Food and Freedom*. Washington, DC: Conference on Economic Progress, (On Deposit, Truman Memorial Presidential Library, Independence, Missouri, USA)

Keyserling, Leon H. (1961) *Jobs and Growth*. Washington, DC: Conference on Economic Progress, (On Deposit, Truman Memorial Presidential Library, Independence, Missouri, USA).

Keyserling, Leon H. (1962) *Poverty and Deprivation in the United States*. Washington, DC: Conference on Economic Progress, (On Deposit, Truman Memorial Presidential Library, Independence, Missouri, USA).

Keyserling, Leon H. (1963) Taxes and the Public Interest. Washington, DC: Conference on Economic Progress, (On Deposit, Truman Memorial Presidential Library, Independence, Missouri, USA).

Keyserling, Leon H. (1964a) *Progress or Poverty*. Washington, DC: Conference on Economic Progress, (On Deposit, Truman Memorial Presidential Library, Independence, Missouri, USA).

Keyserling, Leon H. (1964b) *The Toll of Rising Interest Rates*. Washington, DC: Conference on Economic Progress, (On Deposit, Truman Memorial Presidential Library, Independence, Missouri, USA).

Keyserling, Leon H. (1965) *Agriculture and the Public Interest*. Washington, DC: Conference on Economic Progress, (On Deposit, Truman Memorial Presidential Library, Independence, Missouri, USA).

Keyserling, Leon H. (1966a) *The Role of Wages in a Great Society*. Washington, DC: Conference on Economic Progress, (On Deposit, Truman Memorial Presidential Library, Independence, Missouri, USA).

Keyserling, Leon H. (1966b) *A "Freedom Budget" For All Americans*. Washington, DC: Conference on Economic Progress, (On Deposit, Truman Memorial Presidential Library, Independence, Missouri, USA).

Keyserling, Leon H. (1969) *Taxation of Whom and For What?* Washington, DC: Conference on Economic Progress, (On Deposit, Truman Memorial Presidential Library, Independence, Missouri, USA).

Keyserling, Leon H. (1971) *Wages, Prices, and Profits*. Washington, DC: Conference on Economic Progress, (On Deposit, Truman Memorial Presidential Library, Independence, Missouri, USA).

Keyserling, Leon H. (1972) *The Coming Crisis in Housing*. Washington, DC: Conference on Economic Progress, (On Deposit, Truman Memorial Presidential Library, Independence, Missouri, USA).

Keyserling, Leon H. (1973) *The Scarcity School of Economics: The Shortages it Has Wrought*. Washington, DC: Conference on Economic Progress, (On Deposit, Truman Memorial Presidential Library, Independence, Missouri, USA).

Keyserling, Leon H. (1975) *Full Employment Without Inflation*. Washington, DC: Conference on Economic Progress, (On Deposit, Truman Memorial Presidential Library, Independence, Missouri, USA).

Keyserling, Leon H. (1975) "Full Employment Act by 1976." *Challenge*, July/August: pp. 22–32.

Keyserling, Leon H. (1976) *Toward Full Employment Within Three Years.* Washington, DC: Conference on Economic Progress, (On Deposit, Truman Memorial Presidential Library, Independence, Missouri, USA).

Keyserling, Leon H. (1977) *The Humphrey-Hawkins Bill: Full Employment and Balanced Growth Act of 1977.* Washington, DC: Conference on Economic Progress, (On Deposit, Truman Memorial Presidential Library, Independence, Missouri, USA).

Keyserling, Leon H. (1978) "The Council of Economic Advisers Since 1946: Its Contributions and Failures." *Atlantic Economic Journal*, March: pp. 17–22.

Keyserling, Leon H. (1979) *"Liberal" and "Conservative" National Economic Policies and Their Consequences, 1918–79.* Washington, DC: Conference on Economic Progress, (On Deposit, Truman Memorial Presidential Library, Independence, Missouri, USA).

Keyserling, Leon H. (1980) *Money, Credit, and Interest Rates: Their Gross Mismanagement by the Federal Reserve System.* Washington, DC: Conference on Economic Progress, (On Deposit, Truman Memorial Presidential Library, Independence, Missouri, USA).

Keyserling, Leon H. (1980) "Towards More Realism and Relevance in National Economic Policy." *Atlantic Economic Journal*, March: pp. 17–22.

Keyserling, Leon H. (1983) *How to Cut Unemployment to Four Percent and End Inflation and Deficits By 1987.* Washington, DC: Conference on Economic Progress, (On Deposit, Truman Memorial Presidential Library, Independence, Missouri, USA).

Keyserling, Leon H. (1986) "Let's Get This Straight." *Challenge*, November: pp. 56–8.

Keyserling, Leon H. (1987) "Will it Be Progress or Poverty?" *Challenge*, May/June: pp. 30–6.

Keyserling, Mary Dublin. (1987) "Memories of Leon H. Keyserling," a publication for the Memorial Service for Leon H. Keyserling, Cosmo Club, Washington, DC, September 10. Robert Asher, Chair; and William Keyserling and Mary Dublin Keyserling.

Lewis, John P. (1953) "A Proposal for Work in the Field of Wage-Profit Rlations..." January 19.

Lewis, J., and Schultze, C. (1952) "To the Council." September 29.

McCoy, Donald R. (1984) *The Presidency of Harry S. Truman.* Lawrence, Kansas: University of Kansas Press.

Neikirk, William R. (1987) *Volcker: Portrait of a Money Man.* New York: Congdon And Ward.

Nourse, Edwin G. (1956) "Defining our Employment Goals Under the 1946 Act." *Review of Economics and Statistics*, Vol. 38, May.

Pickens, Donald K. (1975) "Truman's Council of Economic Advisers and the Legacy of New Deal "Liberalism." Truman Memorial Presidential Library, Correspondence Between Truman and Keyserling, 1947–1972, Box 1 of 2.

Pickens, Donald K. "The Council of Economic Advisers and the Cold: The early years." a paper presented to the annual meeting of the organization of American Historians, April, 1975. On Deposit, Dissolution Masters Shelf, Harry S. Truman Library, Independence, Missouri, USA.

Richey, John C. (1977) "We Can Have Full Employment Without Inflation." *St. Petersburg Times*, Sunday, March 27, 3D.

Richey, John C. (1977) Letters, "Wage and Price Control *CAN* Work." *St. Petersburg Times*, April 17.

Samuelson, Paul. (1951) *Principles of Economics*, 2nd edn. New York: Mc-Graw-Hill, pp. 412–19.

Santoni, G.J. (1980) "The Employment Act of 1946: Some History Notes." *Review*, Federal Reserve Bank of St. Louis, Vol. 68, No. 9, November: pp. 5–15.

Schiller, Bradley. (1988) *Newsletter, The Economy Today*. New York: Random House.

Silverman, Corrine. (1959) *The Presidential Economic Advisers*, Intra-University Case Program, #48. University of Alabama: University of Alabama Press.

Tobin, James. (1986) "High Time to Restore the Employment Act of 1946." *Challenge*, May/June: pp. 4–12.

Tugwell, Rexford Guy. (1932) "The Principles of Planning and the Institution of Laissez Faire." *American Economic Review*, Vol. 22, March Supplement: pp. 75–90.

Tugwell, Rexford Guy. (1935 [1924]) *The Trend of Economics*. New York: F.S. Crofts.

Truman, Harry S. (1945) Public Papers of the Presidents, Harry S. Truman, 1945, Sept. 6 (128), pp. 263–307; Special Message to the Congress Presenting a 21-Point Program for the Reconversion Period. Truman Memorial Presidential Library, Independence, Missouri, USA.

United States Congress: Joint Economic Committee of Congress (HJEC, 1949) Hearings on the Economic Report of the President (HCERP). Testimony Of Leon Keyserling (Conference on Economic Progress), February 8–18, pp. 7–130.

United States Congress: Joint Economic Committee of Congress (HJEC, 1952) Testimony of Leon Keyserling, January, pp. 4–37.

United States Congress: Joint Economic Committee of Congress (HJEC, 1951) Testimony of Leon Keyserling, January 24–February 2, pp. 2–37; pp. 273f.

United States Congress: Joint Economic Committee of Congress (HJEC, 1955) Testimony of Leon Keyserling, January 24–February 16, p. 66f; pp. 109–62.

United States Congress: Joint Economic Committee of Congress (HJEC, 1957) Testimony of Leon Keyserling, January 28–February 6, pp. 159–68.

United States Congress: Joint Economic Committee of Congress (HJEC, 1962a) Testimony of Leon Keyserling, January 25–February 8, pp. 553–83.

United States Congress: Joint Economic Committee of Congress (HJEC, 1962b) Testimony of Leon Keyserling, "State of the Economy and Policies for Full Employment," August, pp. 205–92.

United States Congress: Joint Economic Committee of Congress (HJEC, 1963) Testimony of Leon Keyserling, January 28–February 6, Part 2, pp. 698–766.

United States Congress: Joint Economic Committee of Congress (HJEC, 1964) Testimony of Leon Keyserling, February, Part 2, pp. 63–110.

United States Congress: Joint Economic Committee of Congress (HJEC, 1965) Testimony of Leon Keyserling, February 25–27, Part 3, pp. 94–133.

United States Congress: Joint Economic Committee of Congress (HJEC, 1966) Twentieth Anniversary of the Employment Act of 1946, An Economic Symposium, February 23; Testimony of Leon Keyserling, pp. 19–26, 77–86.

United States Congress: Joint Economic Committee of Congress (HJEC, 1976) "Thirtieth Anniversary of the Employment Act of 1946, A National Conference on Full Employment," May 18–19, Testimony of Leon Keyserling, pp. 298–307.

United States Congress: Joint Economic Committee of Congress (HJEC, 1977) Testimony of Leon Keyserling, February 10, pp. 23–24, 419–63.

United States Congress: Joint Economic Committee of Congress (HJEC, 1979) Testimony of Leon Keyserling, February 22–March 8, Part 3, pp. 48–61.

United States Congress: Joint Economic Committee of Congress (HJEC, 1980) Testimony of Leon Keyserling, January 30–February 1, pp. 205–43.

United States Congress: Joint Economic Committee of Congress (HJEC, 1981) Testimony of Leon Keyserling, February 5–20, Part 2, pp. 50–97.

United States Congress: Joint Economic Committee of Congress (HJEC, 1984) Testimony of Leon Keyserling, February 21–28, Part 2, pp. 61–113.

United States Congress: Joint Economic Committee of Congress (1978) Sub-Committee on International Economics (SCIE), Testimony of Leon Keyserling, Dec. 14–15, pp. 69–111.

United States Congress: (1985) Committee on Education and Labor (CEL), Sub-Committee on Employment Opportunities (SCEO), Hearings on the "Income and Jobs Action Act of 1985," Testimony of Leon Keyserling, pp. 63–80.

United States Congress: (CEL, 1986) "Oversight Hearing on the Full Employment and Balanced Growth Act of 1978," Testimony of Leon Keyserling, pp. 12–53.

Virgo, John M. (1987) "Leon H. Keyserling, 1908–1987." *Atlantic Economic Journal*, (Atlantic Economic Society), September: p. 1.

Wehmeyer, Willadee Gillan. (1994) A dissertation. *Mary Dublin Keyserling: Economist and Social Activist.* Kansas City, Missouri: University of Missouri-Kansas City.

Weidenbaum, Murray L. (1976) "The Case Against the Humphrey-Hawkins Bill." *Challenge Magazine*, September/October: pp. 21–23.

Index